INSPIRATIONAL STORIES *for* PURPOSEFUL LIVING - 1

150 Stories That Live and Teach

For Speakers, Teachers and Value Instructors

JOHN PARANKIMALIL

INDIA • SINGAPORE • MALAYSIA

ISBN 979-8-89233-589-8

CONTENTS

FOREWORD

Storytelling is one of humanity's oldest and most powerful traditions. Stories can inspire and transform, conveying wisdom, life lessons, and glimpses into diverse lives and experiences. This compelling collection of 150 stories continues that rich tradition of storytelling, aimed at uplifting, educating, and helping us reflect on our journeys.

Spanning genres from historical tales to biographies and modern parables, the stories tackle diverse themes but share a common thread of imparting insight and inspiration. Some narratives highlight the persevering human spirit in the face of formidable odds, while others explore profound realisations that led to personal growth. Readers will uncover stories of compassion meeting cruelty, the far-reaching influence of childhood experiences, the triumphs of unlocking one's true potential, and the quiet but heroic acts of daily sacrifice.

From a soldier's demonstration of empathy on the battlefield to a child's lesson in seeing the wonders in everyday life, the stories bind us in our shared experiences of love, loss, courage, and transformation. They remind us that progress often comes from the right response to adversity and examine the rippling impacts of integrity, understanding, and living purposefully. Readers will uncover eternal virtues and timeworn wisdom but also modern applications to current challenges.

Inspirational Stories for Purposeful Living – 1 & 2 by John Parankimalil, an accomplished storyteller, offers thought-provoking stories to return to again and again. It provides glimpses into the lives of notable individuals, achievers, historical figures, and characters from popular movies. The book contains stories of resilience and triumph from various walks of life, narratives inspired by the achievements and challenges of famous personalities, tales that reflect on spiritual awakening, innovation, and leadership, stories demonstrating the power of determination, perseverance, and vision, accounts emphasising the importance of ethics, humility, and compassion. Each story in the book is intended to motivate and encourage readers to reach for their highest ideals. Most importantly, these narratives illustrate the power of stories themselves to change how we perceive our world and live our lives. I congratulate the author and appreciate his labour of love accomplished with great commitment and passion. May these volumes inspire the readers to rekindle the humane values to serve their fellow human beings with greater zest!

Dr. (Fr) Joy Kachappilly, SDB
Rector, Assam Don Bosco University,
Azara Campus, Guwahati, India

INTRODUCTION

As Rudyard Kipling eloquently stated, "If history were taught in the form of stories, it would never be forgotten." Stories have long captivated our minds, hearts, and imaginations, possessing unparalleled power to convey messages in a uniquely memorable way.

In our modern age of information overload, technological dependence, and the pervasive demand for speed, it is stories that linger in our memory. By bringing abstract lessons to life, stories facilitate profound "aha" moments, promote self-reflection, and reveal how we can best leverage our talents to contribute meaningfully to the world.

Stories speak directly to the heart, eliciting powerful emotions that refresh the soul. Through compelling narratives, we uncover truths about life that facts alone cannot convey. The stories in this collection take readers by the hand, engage the mind, tug at the heartstrings, and demonstrate what is possible.

Why Stories?

The appeal of a good story is universal. Stories impart clarity to complex ideas while imbuing them with compelling interest. An impactful speech invariably contains strategic references to jokes, quotes, personal anecdotes and family histories. I believe stories serve several vital functions:

- Stories attract and sustain interest, making even difficult subjects relatable and memorable.

- Listeners identify with story characters, absorbing messaging intuitively.
- Stories aid recall where the volume of information poses a challenge.
- Key points, conveyed through multiple apt stories, reinforce messaging without sounding repetitive.
- By eliciting emotion, stories spark interest far more than impersonal instructions can achieve.

These stories are based on the lives of notable individuals, achievers, historical figures, and characters from popular movies. The book contains:

- Stories of resilience and triumph from various walks of life.
- Narratives inspired by the achievements and challenges of famous personalities.
- Tales that reflect on spiritual awakening, innovation, and leadership.
- Stories demonstrating the power of determination, perseverance, and vision.

Accounts emphasising the importance of ethics, humility, and compassion.

Each story in the book is intended to motivate and encourage readers to reach for their highest ideals.

Sources of Stories

Seasoned orators advise keen observation of daily events as a rich source of diverse stories. However, it is equally worthwhile to gather stories from books, the internet, and other people's experiences. The chosen stories should complement the topic and contain relatable insights or lessons for the audience.

When including stories from your own life, ensure accuracy regarding facts and sequencing. Even if aliases are used, distorted personal accounts can undermine credibility and leave you struggling to address follow-up questions. Fictional tales allow more artistic licence but should still be narrated consistently.

Over decades, I have collected stories from sources including:

- Newspapers, magazines, journals, and periodicals
- YouTube, social media
- Best-selling books and popular fiction
- Radio shows, podcasts, videos
- Movies and television
- TED talks
- Speeches and sermons
- Business seminars and leadership conferences
- Biographies and life stories of influential figures

I have crafted a collection of stories that draw inspiration from the lives of extraordinary individuals, both past and present. These narratives feature achievers who have made significant marks in history, heroes, and remarkable men and women whose experiences offer motivation and encouragement to the current generation. Additionally, I have woven tales inspired by iconic Indian cinema, designed to inspire and motivate people through the powerful medium of storytelling. These stories serve as a beacon, illuminating the path for those seeking guidance and inspiration in their own lives.

This list is not exhaustive but provides a glimpse into the multitude of platforms offering insightful narratives. While accessing all potential sources may be unrealistic, maintaining an open and curious orientation can uncover inspiring stories in unexpected places.

Familiarity With the Story

Before including a story, ensure thorough familiarity with the details. When drawing from personal experience, accuracy matters. Even with aliases, fabricated elements could invite doubt or necessitate tedious explanations. Similarly, faithfulness to the original version retains the integrity of curated stories.

Of course, this expectation of precision does not apply to fictional tales. However, consistency in the retelling of imagined stories enables crisp delivery and audience engagement. Masterful orators know their chosen stories intimately, seamlessly conveying emotive undercurrents through vocal inflection, body language, and facial expressions.

Theme-Based Stories

Avoid the temptation to include stories merely intended to entertain. Each story must tie directly into the core theme of the speech. Tangential narratives, no matter how amusing, serve only as distractions without reinforcing central messaging. Skillful speakers intentionally select stories that shed light on key points or crystallise important ideas.

Resist making strained connections or justifying a story's relevance. If explaining the relationship requires effort, opt for a different story whose linkage is self-evident. Audiences lose focus attempting to draw meaning from obscure threads. Search for stories where the inherent moral or lesson aligns cleanly with your topic.

Using Emotions

When narrating stories, simply describing pivotal moments falls short of potential impact. Imbue the retelling with suitable emotions – not merely those overtly stated but also the unspoken yet contextually evident undercurrents. Let your voice, expressions, and gestures mirror the atmosphere to transport listeners fully into each scene. While demanding practice, dedicated emotional attunement rewards through audience engagement and recall.

In closing, may the stories, morals, and quotes gathered in this anthology enrich your collections. With regular use, these narratives will surely hone public speaking prowess, sparking interest and leaving positive impressions. I welcome reader feedback and suggestions to refine future editions of this work. Let's collectively cultivate our innate love of stories into a means for change.

John Parankimalil
Author

1. THE WILL TO RISE

"Our greatest weakness lies in giving up. The most certain way to succeed is always to try just one more time." – Thomas A. Edison

As a young girl, Rukmani faced a significant setback when she failed Class VI. This failure brought disappointment from her parents, ridicule from her friends, and scepticism from her neighbours and relatives. Everyone around her was quick to judge and label her as lacking intelligence. Suggestions poured in to send her for tuition, but Rukmani knew the truth behind her failure—it wasn't a lack of intelligence, but a lack of effort and focus.

Instead of succumbing to the pressure and criticism, Rukmani took a bold stand. She rejected the idea of tuition and decided to challenge herself. Determined to turn her life around, she committed to working hard and giving her best in her studies. This decision marked the beginning of a remarkable transformation.

Her efforts paid off. Not only did she never fail again, but she also excelled in her academic pursuits. She passed her secondary and higher secondary examinations with high percentages, and during her college studies, she won gold medals—twice. Her academic journey peaked when she graduated from the Tata Institute of Social Sciences in Mumbai.

Rukmani's ambition didn't stop there. She set her sights on the Indian Administrative Service (IAS), one of the most prestigious and challenging competitive exams in India. Remarkably, she cleared the IAS in her first attempt, and without any coaching, secured the second rank in the country in 2011. Rukmani Riar, once a student who failed in Class VI, had become an IAS topper—a testament to the power of determination, hard work, and perseverance.

***

Rukmani Riar's journey from failure to IAS topper is a powerful reminder that setbacks are not the end but a chance to realign and rise. Let her story inspire us to embrace challenges, trust in our capabilities, and persevere through adversity. Remember, it's not how we fall, but how we rise that defines our journey. Embrace every obstacle as an opportunity to grow stronger and achieve greatness.

2. THE OLD MECHANIC'S INSIGHT

"If I had an hour to solve a problem, I'd spend 55 minutes thinking about the problem and 5 minutes thinking about solutions." – Albert Einstein

A ship at sea faced a daunting challenge: a technical snag in its engine that left it stranded in a harbour. The onboard engineers, despite their best efforts, couldn't fix the problem. They urgently sought an expert, particularly one skilled in handling older engines, as their ship was quite ancient.

Finally, they found an old mechanic, known for his exceptional skill and equally high charges. Without hesitation, he was invited aboard to tackle the engine issue. The mechanic arrived with just a few tools – a set of spanners and a hammer. He meticulously inspected the engine, his years of experience guiding him. Then, he did something astonishingly simple yet effective. With precise taps of his hammer on a specific part of the engine, he miraculously fixed the problem. The engine roared back to life, much to everyone's amazement. The entire process took less than an hour.

When it came time to settle the bill, the old mechanic's charge was £10,000. The captain, stunned by the hefty fee for such a brief job, demanded an itemised bill. Obliging, the mechanic provided a detailed invoice: "£1 for tapping thrice with the hammer; £9,999 for knowing where to tap." A total of £10,000.

***

The old mechanic's story teaches us the true value of experience and knowledge. It's not just about the time spent on a task, but the years of learning and understanding that lead to the solution. Let this story remind us to value and respect the wisdom that comes with experience, and to recognise that sometimes, the simplest solutions are born from a lifetime of dedication and insight.

3. TRUST AMIDST THE TURBULENCE

"Trust is the glue of life. It's the foundational principle that holds all relationships." – Stephen R. Covey

On a long flight from Hong Kong to New York, a calm announcement from the stewardess filled the cabin, instructing passengers to remain seated due to expected turbulence. The plane soon found itself amidst a fierce storm, with thunder roaring and lightning flashing against the dark skies, rattling even the most seasoned travellers.

In the midst of this chaos, a man sitting next to a little girl was gripped by a panic attack, his fear exacerbated by the turbulent flight. As he struggled with his anxiety, he noticed the girl calmly reading a book beside him, seemingly unaffected by the storm. Astonished, he asked her how she could remain so composed under such terrifying circumstances.

The girl looked up from her book with a smile and said, "Don't be afraid, Mister." The man, still shaken, questioned further, "Aren't you afraid while we fly through such a terrible storm?" Her response was both simple and profound: "Sir, the pilot is my dad, and he is taking me home."

Her words struck a chord with the man. The girl's unshakeable trust in her father, the pilot, instilled in her a sense of safety and calm amidst the chaos. Her confidence in her father's abilities to steer them through the storm provided her with an inner peace that was contagious.

***

Like the pilot's daughter, let us find strength in trust during life's turbulent times. Her unwavering belief in her father's guidance is a reminder that faith in those who led us can be our anchor amidst chaos. Embrace trust as a beacon of calm, allowing it to transform fear into assurance. May her story inspire us to seek and find peace in trusting relationships, weathering storms with confidence and grace.

4. LIFE WITHOUT LIMITS

"Fear is the biggest disability of all. And will paralyse you more than being in a wheelchair." – *Nick Vujicic*

Nick Vujicic's life story is a remarkable testament to the human spirit's resilience and the power of hope. Born with tetra-amelia syndrome, Nick lacked arms and legs, a condition that presented unimaginable challenges. As a child, he faced not only physical limitations but also emotional turmoil, including bullying at school and a profound sense of despair.

At the tender age of 10, Nick's pain was so overwhelming that he contemplated suicide. However, the thought of his parents' grief stopped him. His life took a pivotal turn at 17 when he read about a disabled man who refused to let his condition dictate his life. This inspired Nick to shift his focus from what he lacked to the blessings he had.

Nick's transformation was profound. He embraced his unique journey and founded 'Life Without Limbs,' a non-profit organisation. He became a renowned motivational speaker and best-selling author, touching millions of lives with his message of hope and perseverance. In 2008, Nick's life blossomed further when he met his future wife, leading to a loving marriage and the joy of 4 children.

He engages in activities like painting, swimming, skydiving, surfing, and playing golf, exemplifying that limitations are often self-imposed. Nick Vujicic's life is a powerful reminder that with faith, courage, and a positive mindset, one can lead a fulfilling and limitless life, regardless of circumstances.

***

Nick Vujicic's incredible journey from despair to global inspiration exemplifies that true limitations are in the mind, not the body. His resilience and zest for life teach us that purpose and happiness are attainable, regardless of our challenges. Nick's story is not just about overcoming physical disabilities; it's about breaking free from mental and emotional shackles. Remember, it's not the absence of struggles that defines us, but how we choose to respond to them.

5. CHOOSING POSITIVITY IN A NEGATIVE WORLD

"Only I can change my life. No one can do it for me."
– Carol Burnett

Once upon a time, in the hustle and bustle of life, a man named David embarked on a journey that would change his perspective forever. David found himself in a taxi, en route to the airport. Little did he know, this ordinary taxi ride would unfold into an extraordinary life lesson. As the taxi cruised at a normal speed, a red car hastily emerged, narrowly avoiding a collision. Tires screeched, hearts raced, and anger brewed. The furious driver of the red car confronted the taxi driver. Instead of reacting impulsively, the middle-aged taxi driver simply smiled and waved.

Puzzled, David questioned the taxi driver about his calm response. With a smile, the driver shared his profound life philosophy. "Sir, many people are like overflowing garbage bins. When they try to throw their negativity onto you, don't take it personally. Smile, wave, and continue on your path."

This real-life story inspired David J Polley to pen down his experiences in a book titled "The Law of the Garbage Truck," encapsulating three key lessons. 1. Choose Understanding Over Reaction: Life will present situations where others may unload their negativity onto you. Instead of reacting impulsively, respond with understanding and calmness. 2. Balance Your Responses: The taxi driver's choice to smile and wave exemplifies choosing a balanced response over a reactionary one. 3. Prioritise Your Well-being: Your mental and emotional well-being should be your top priority. Don't let someone else's bad day impact your own. Maintain boundaries and choose positivity.

***

Empty your mind of negativity and consciously fill it with positive emotions—love, gratefulness, and overall positivity. Even if it overflows, it's okay; let it radiate. As you navigate through life, remember "The Law of the Garbage Truck." Choose positivity, prioritise your well-being, and let the overflowing positivity in your mind brighten the world around you. This unexpected life lesson turned into a powerful philosophy, a reminder that in a world full of negativity, we have the choice to respond with love, understanding, and a smile.

6. THE LITTLE GIRL WITH A BIG HEART

"A single act of kindness throws out roots in all directions, and the roots spring up and make new trees." – Amelia Earhart

In this fast-paced world, consumed by technology and social media, it's easy to lose sight of what really matters – people and connections. The story of 12-year-old Hope Elizabeth Stout reminds us that one person with a big heart can make a huge difference.

In 2003, Hope was diagnosed with a rare bone cancer. The Make-A-Wish Foundation offered her a wish, but instead of asking for something for herself, Hope wished that the other 155 children waiting for wishes could have theirs granted first. She selflessly asked that it be done by January 16, 2004.

When told it wasn't possible to grant so many wishes so quickly, Hope was disappointed but undeterred. She turned her dismay into enthusiasm, inspiring others to raise the over $1 million needed. Hope's story spread through newspapers, radio, and TV. Her pure desire to help others touched hearts everywhere. Schools, businesses, and organizations came together to make Hope's wish a reality.

Though she passed away on January 4th, knowing her wish would come true was a great comfort to Hope. On January 16th, the anniversary of her wish, it was announced that over $1 million had been raised for the children. Hope's wish had come true!

***

Hope's story teaches us so much about what really matters. In a world where we're bombarded by negative news, and self-interest seems to rule, Hope's selflessness shines like a beacon of light. This brave young girl saw beyond her own needs and found joy in helping others. Hope shows us that when we come together for the greater good, amazing things can happen. The dashes on our tombstones represent the time we spend on earth. Hope chose to fill her dash by giving joy to others, despite her own challenges. She created a lasting legacy by touching so many lives. Though her time was far too short, Hope inspired people of all ages. Her memory continues to encourage others to give, love and make a difference.

7. ALEXANDER'S FINAL LESSONS

"Remember that your real wealth can be measured not by what you have, but by what you are." – Napoleon Hill

As Alexander the Great, the Macedonian King who had conquered vast lands, lay on his deathbed, he was struck by a profound realisation. He understood that despite his immense power and wealth, he couldn't fulfil a simple desire to see his mother's face one last time. In his final moments, he summoned his generals and expressed 3 wishes that he wanted to be carried out.

His first wish was that only his physicians should carry his coffin. Secondly, he desired that the path to his grave be strewn with gold, silver, and precious stones from his treasury. Lastly, he wanted his hands to be left dangling outside his coffin.

When questioned about these peculiar wishes, Alexander revealed the lessons he had learned. He wanted the world to know that even the best physicians are powerless against death, highlighting the inevitability and impartiality of mortality. His second wish was to show that despite a lifetime of accumulating wealth, he could not take a fraction of it with him, emphasising the futility of material greed. Finally, by having his hands exposed, he wanted to symbolise that he entered and would leave this world empty-handed, underscoring the transient nature of worldly possessions and status.

***

Alexander the Great's final lessons remind us that life's true value lies not in wealth or conquests, but in the humility and wisdom we acquire. His wishes at death's door serve as a powerful reminder of our shared human fate: no matter how great, we all face the same end. Let's focus on what truly matters – compassion, understanding, and the legacy of kindness we leave behind.

8. A MOTHER'S DIGNIFIED DUTY

"There is no role in life that is more essential than that of motherhood." – Elder M. Russell Ballard

When street sweeper Sumitra Devi retired after 30 years, few noticed the unremarkable ceremony. But then came a cavalcade of vehicles carrying 3 influential men who stunned the gathering by touching Sumitra's feet in deep respect. They were Mahendra, a district collector; Virendra, a railway engineer; and Dhirendra, a doctor. All 3 were Sumitra's sons.

They explained: "We lost our father early on and knew hardship until our mother secured work as a street cleaner. She laboured tirelessly so we had food, shelter and education. When we grew up and became successful, she declined to stop working, as it allowed her to support us when we needed it most."

Sumitra added tearfully: "I cannot leave something that turned my dreams of educating my boys into reality. My duty was to raise them well through hard work. How could I relinquish this dignified work that gave everything to my family?"

Despite her influential sons pleading her to stop, Sumitra cherished her essential role that paved the way for their ascent. Though sweeping streets, she walked with head held high, proud that her sacrifices granted her children better lives. Her story teaches that no honest work should be looked down upon, for labourers everywhere strive to build better futures. And nothing is more honourable than toiling for family – the bedrock of civilisation.

***

All labour that builds futures deserves dignity. No role more sacred exists than motherhood's selfless dedication so children can attain meaningful lives. For their triumphs are ours, and their joys are our greatest rewards. Sumitra Devi has shown that no job is degrading, or small if done with honesty and dedication. Work is worship. If a job gives you employment, and helps you to create opportunities for others, it's indeed a noble deed and you should take pride in doing it.

9. THE POWER OF APPRECIATION

"There is more hunger for love and appreciation in this world than for bread." – Mother Teresa

The movie "Stand and Deliver" features Jaime Escalante, a dedicated mathematics teacher at Garfield High School from 1974 to 1991. In his class were 2 students, both named Johnny, who were in stark contrast to each other. One was an exemplary student, a leader and a role model, always engaged and helpful. The other Johnny was the opposite: dishevelled, unresponsive, frequently late, and disruptive.

During a parent-teacher event, a woman, introducing herself as Johnny's mother, inquired about her son's performance. Assuming she was the mother of the high-achieving Johnny, Escalante enthusiastically praised her son's contributions to the class. He expressed his wish to have more students like him.

The next day, something remarkable happened. The troubled Johnny arrived on time, with his homework completed, actively participating and engaging in the class. This transformation was noticed by everyone. After the class, he approached Escalante and, with a soft voice, thanked him for wanting him in the class. The teacher's words, meant for another but received by him, had made a profound impact. From that day forward, Johnny became one of the most remarkable students Escalante ever taught. This accidental act of recognition and appreciation had turned Johnny's life around, showing the power of positive reinforcement and belief in a student's potential.

***

Johnny's story is a powerful reminder of how recognition and belief can transform lives. A simple act of appreciation, even if unintentional, can ignite a spark of change. It is said, "Believe in someone, and they have the power to become what you perceive." As educators and mentors, our words carry immense power. Let us use them to uplift and inspire, to bring out the best in each individual, for sometimes, all a student needs is to know that someone believes in them.

10. PAID WITH A GLASS OF MILK

"To do more for the world than the world does for you – that is success." – Henry Ford

In a small town, a poor boy selling goods door-to-door to fund his education found himself with just a dime left and a gnawing hunger. At one house, a beautiful young woman answered his timid knock. Too nervous to ask for food, he requested a glass of water. Sensing his hunger, she returned with a generous glass of milk.

Gratefully, he drank and asked, "How much do I owe you?" Her response was kind and firm, "Nothing. We never accept payment for kindness." His heart warmed by this act, left that place with renewed physical strength and a fortified faith in both God and humanity, vowing to succeed.

Years passed, and the woman fell critically ill with a rare disease. Local doctors were stumped and sent her to a city hospital for specialist care. There, Dr. Howard Kelly, a renowned physician, was called for consultation. Learning of her hometown, a spark of recognition lit his eyes. He visited her, immediately recognising the kind woman from his past.

Determined to save her, Dr. Kelly devoted special attention to her case. After an arduous battle, she recovered. When the final bill was prepared, Dr. Kelly personally reviewed it, writing something on the margin before sending it to her room.

Trembling with fear at the expected cost, the woman hesitantly opened the bill. Her eyes were drawn to the note on the side: "Paid in full with one glass of milk. Signed, Dr. Howard Kelly."

***

The story of the glass of milk illustrates the profound impact of kindness. It is said, "Kindness, like a boomerang, always returns." A simple act of compassion can ripple through time, returning in unexpected and miraculous ways. It teaches us that every gesture of generosity, no matter how small, holds the power to transform lives. Let this story inspire us to always practise kindness, for we never know how our actions might echo into the future, changing lives in ways we could never imagine.

11. NEVER JUDGE ANYONE

"People who judge others tell more about who they are, than who they judge." – Donald L. Hicks, Look into the stillness

A doctor rushed to the hospital for an urgent surgery. Upon his arrival, he encountered the patient's anxious father, who rebuked him for the delay, questioning his sense of responsibility. The doctor, with a calm demeanour, apologised for his late arrival, explaining he came as quickly as possible and urged the father to remain calm for the surgery's sake.

The father, in his distress, further questioned the doctor's empathy, asking if he would remain calm if it were his own son in such a perilous situation. The doctor replied with a gentle smile, emphasising the importance of hope and prayer in times of crisis.

After hours of surgery, the doctor emerged, relieved, announcing the success of the operation to the father. Without waiting for a response, he quickly left, advising the father to seek any further information from the nursing staff.

The father, taken aback by the doctor's perceived aloofness, expressed his dissatisfaction to a nurse. It was then that the tragic truth came to light. The nurse, with tears streaming down her face, revealed that the doctor's own son had passed away in a road accident the day before. He had been attending his son's burial when the call for the surgery came. After saving the father's son, he rushed back to complete his child's burial.

***

I have heard it said, "Before you assume, learn the facts. Before you judge, understand why. Before you hurt someone, feel. Before you speak, think." No one has the right to judge anyone because you never know how their life is and what they're going through. It only takes a few seconds to hurt people you love, and it can take years to heal. Let this story inspire us to be more compassionate, recognising the silent battles others may be fighting, while selflessly offering their help to those in need.

12. YOU FIND WHAT YOU'RE LOOKING FOR

"We find whatever it is we're looking for. Look for the good." – AL Carraway

In the harsh deserts of North America, 2 types of birds fly at the same height, speed, and environment, yet their perspectives and reactions differ vastly. One is the vulture, and the other is the hummingbird.

The vulture thrives in the desert by feeding on decomposing meat. It searches the barren landscape for carcasses, flourishing on a diet derived from death and decay. Its life revolves around finding sustenance in the remnants of what once was, focusing solely on the negative aspects of its environment.

In stark contrast, the hummingbird seems oblivious to the desert's desolation. It does not notice the stench of rotting flesh or the lifeless scenery. Instead, this tiny bird seeks out the beautiful blossoms of cactus plants. Amidst the dry, parched land, it finds vibrant flowers and sips nectar, sustaining itself with life-affirming sweetness. Moreover, the hummingbird enjoys the fresh waters of the desert's rare oases, finding nourishment and refreshment in the most unlikely places.

Both birds find what they look for in the same environment. The vulture sees death and decay, while the hummingbird sees life and nourishment. Their perspectives shape their experiences, demonstrating how focus and attitude can determine one's reality even in identical circumstances.

***

The tale of the vulture and the hummingbird teaches us about perspective. In the same environment, one finds decay while the other finds beauty. This story reminds us that our focus determines our reality. Let's choose to be like the hummingbird, seeking out the positive and nourishing aspects of our lives, even in challenging conditions. Our perspective has the power to transform our experiences, turning even a desert into a place of beauty and sustenance.

13. KEEP BURNING BRIGHTLY

"Burn brightly without burning out. Throw your heart over the fence and the rest will follow. Keep your face to the sunshine and you won't see the shadows." — Helen Keller

One evening, a man took a small candle from a box and began ascending a long, winding stairway. The candle, curious and somewhat apprehensive, asked, "Where are we going?" The man replied, "We're climbing up to the lighthouse to guide ships to the harbour."

Doubtful of its significance, the candle lamented, "But no ship in the harbour will ever see my light. It is so very small." The man, with a reassuring tone, advised, "If your light is small, just keep burning as brightly as you can, and leave the rest to me."

Upon reaching the top of the stairs, they arrived at a grand lamp. The man carefully lit this lamp with the small candle. Suddenly, the large, polished mirrors behind the lamp magnified the candle's light, sending powerful beams across miles of sea. This brilliant light, originating from the humble flame of the small candle, became the guiding beacon for ships navigating their way to the harbour.

This journey of the candle from a box to become the source of light for the lamp at the lighthouse is symbolic. It demonstrates that even the smallest contribution, when placed in the right context and combined with other forces, can have a tremendous impact. The candle's light, seemingly insignificant on its own, became essential in guiding ships safely to their destination.

***

The story of the candle's light reminds us that no effort is too small, and every contribution matters. Even the faintest light can lead the way when amplified with support and belief. This tale encourages us to keep shining our light, however modest it may seem, for in the right circumstances, it can make a profound difference. "A small spark can start a great fire." Let's remember that our small actions can have a significant impact when aligned with a greater purpose.

14. MOTHERS CAN CHANGE THE DESTINY OF A CHILD

> *"A mother is one who can take the place of all others but whose place no one else can take." – Cardinal Mermillod*

Thomas Edison, one of history's most prolific inventors, once came home with a letter from his teacher, given to him to pass on to his mother. His mother, with tears in her eyes, read the letter aloud to her young son. The letter proclaimed, "Your son is a genius. This school is too small for him and doesn't have enough good teachers for training him. Please teach him yourself."

Years passed, and Edison's mother passed away. By then, Edison had become one of the greatest inventors of the century, credited with numerous inventions that transformed the world. One day, while rummaging through an old closet, he found the very same letter, now worn and faded. Curiosity piqued, he unfolded the letter and read its true content. To his astonishment, the message from his teacher was starkly different: "Your son is mentally ill. We cannot let him attend our school anymore. He is expelled."

Emotional upon discovering the truth, Edison realised the profound impact of his mother's faith in him. Despite the teacher's harsh judgement, his mother chose to see and nurture his potential, forever changing the course of his life. In his diary, Edison penned a heartfelt entry: "Thomas Alva

Edison was a mentally ill child whose mother turned him into the genius of the century."

***

The story of Thomas Edison and his mother teaches us the power of belief and encouragement. Edison's mother saw beyond the limitations imposed by others and chose to believe in her son's potential. Her unwavering faith transformed Edison's life, proving that what we believe about ourselves can shape our destiny. Let this story inspire us to see beyond perceived limitations and to believe in the potential within each of us, for it is in belief that greatness is nurtured.

15. THE VALUE OF SILENCE

"The quieter you become, the more you can hear." – Ram Dass

Once, a farmer lost his cherished gold watch in his expansive barn. This timepiece held not only monetary value but also sentimental significance. Despite a thorough search amidst the hay, the farmer's efforts were in vain. In a bid to find his treasured watch, he enlisted the help of some children playing nearby, promising them a reward for its discovery.

The eager children scurried into the barn, rummaging through and around the vast stacks of hay. Their search, however, was fruitless. They could not locate the watch. As the farmer prepared to surrender to his loss, a young boy from the neighbourhood requested a chance to try. Intrigued, the farmer agreed.

The boy entered the barn and, after 20 minutes, emerged triumphantly, the gold watch in hand. The farmer, astonished, asked how the boy succeeded where others had failed. The boy's answer was simple yet profound. He explained, "All I did was sit quietly on the ground and listen. In the silence, I heard the ticking of your watch and just looked for it in that direction, finding it immediately."

The boy's approach – opting for stillness and attentiveness in contrast to the frantic searching of others – proved to be the key. His wisdom in choosing silence allowed him to perceive what the others could not: the faint yet distinct ticking of the lost watch.

***

The story of the lost watch and the wise boy teaches us the power of silence and attentiveness. Amidst the chaos and noise, sometimes all it takes to find what we seek is to be still and listen. This tale is a reminder to embrace quiet moments, for they can bring clarity and solutions that elude us in the hustle of daily life. In the words of Lao Tzu, "Silence is a source of great strength." Let's remember, in silence, we often find the answers we've been searching for.

16. ENJOY THE TASTE AND FLAVOUR OF LIFE

"If you don't build your dream, someone else will hire you to help them build theirs." – Tony Gaskins

A group of successful alumni visited their old university professor. The conversation soon turned to their stress in work and life. To offer some comfort, the professor prepared coffee for his guests. He returned with a large pot and an assortment of cups—some porcelain, some plastic, some plain, others expensive and exquisite. He invited them to help themselves to the coffee.

As the students each picked a cup and filled it with coffee, the professor noted an interesting choice: all the attractive, expensive cups were selected first, leaving behind the plain and inexpensive ones. He then shared a profound observation: "You all wanted the best for yourselves, which is normal. Yet, that's the source of your stress and problems. What you really wanted was coffee, not the cup, but you unconsciously went for the better cups and now you're comparing each other's cups."

The professor's analogy extended further. He likened life to the coffee and the jobs, money, and position in society to the cups. He explained that these are merely tools to hold and contain life, but they do not change the quality of life itself. Focusing too much on the 'cups' can make us fail to enjoy the 'coffee' within.

"Don't let the cups drive you," he advised. "Enjoy the coffee."

***

The story of the coffee cups teaches us a valuable lesson about priorities and contentment. In our pursuit of the best 'cups,' we often lose sight of the 'coffee'—the essence of life itself. This story reminds us to focus on what truly matters, to cherish the experiences and people that enrich our lives, rather than getting caught up in materialistic comparisons. "Life is like a cup of coffee. It's all about how you make or take it." Let's savour the coffee of life, appreciating its richness, regardless of the cups we hold.

17. RESPECTING THE ELDERLY

"The elders are the history and mirror of the living past. Study them to brighten your life and future."
– Ehsan Sehgal

On an aeroplane, a rich young woman found herself seated next to a poor elderly man. Uncomfortable with her seating arrangement, she beckoned the flight attendant and demanded another seat, refusing to travel beside someone she deemed a "worthless bum." The economy class was fully booked, but she insisted on a change.

In response, the flight attendant consulted with the captain and returned with a solution. To the woman's expectation, the attendant announced that a seat in first class was available. The woman, smugly preparing to move, was taken aback when the attendant extended the offer to the elderly man instead, apologising for the inconvenience caused by having to travel with such an unpleasant person. The entire plane applauded as the elderly man was escorted to first class, leaving the young woman in utter embarrassment.

This incident served as a poignant lesson in humility and respect. The young woman's sense of entitlement and prejudice against the elderly man was starkly contrasted by the crew's discerning and compassionate decision. It highlighted the importance of treating all individuals, regardless of their apparent social or economic status, with dignity and kindness.

***

The story from the aeroplane teaches us a valuable lesson in humility and respect. It reminds us that wealth and status should never be grounds for belittling others. True character is revealed not in how we treat those who can do something for us, but in how we treat those who seemingly cannot. Let us strive to treat everyone with the dignity and respect they deserve, for every person holds intrinsic value regardless of their external circumstances.

18. THE POWER OF ONE EXTRA DEGREE

"To achieve great things, you must stretch your beliefs, your efforts, and your tolerance." – Brian Cagney

In the quaint town of Persistence, there lived a young dreamer named Alex. One day, Alex stumbled upon a mysterious book by Sam Parker titled "212 Degree: The extra degree." Intrigued, they delved into its pages and discovered a powerful concept.

"At 211 degrees, water is hot. At 212 degrees, it boils. With boiling water, comes steam, and with steam, you can power a locomotive. It's that one extra degree that makes all the difference." The realisation struck Alex like lightning—sometimes, the smallest effort makes the biggest impact. Inspired, Alex embraced the extra degree in every aspect of life.

As days turned into months, Alex's determination reached a boiling point. They poured that extra degree into their passion, work, and relationships. Slowly but surely, the once lukewarm existence transformed into a locomotive of success, powered by the energy of that one additional degree of effort.

The message echoed through the hills of Persistence: Every extra effort counts; it's the difference between standing still and propelling forward. Alex's story became a beacon of motivation, reminding everyone that a single degree can unleash unimaginable power.

***

It's always the extra that gives you the edge. In life, it's one extra degree of effort that separates the good from the great, the hero from the ordinary. Small efforts, consistently applied, create monumental results. Let your journey be fuelled by the power of that one extra degree. It may be 212 service, attitude, leadership, quality, study, smile, reading…that makes you powerful and different! It's time to turn up the heat! The extra degree will show you how one extra degree makes all the difference in everything you do.

19. THE ESSENCE OF DETACHMENT

"Detachment is not that you should own nothing. But that nothing should own you." – Ali ibn abi Talib

In the corridors of power, amidst the allure of international gifts, Dr. APJ Abdul Kalam, the revered President of India, stood as a beacon of humility and detachment. Revealed in the pages of "Kalam Effect" by Mr. PM Nair, the narrative unfolds with a unique practice of the People's President.

Whenever Dr. Kalam received costly gifts during his foreign visits, a customary gesture for heads of state, he embraced them graciously. Yet, what set him apart was his profound detachment from material possessions. Rather than basking in the luxury of these offerings, he chose a different path.

Dr. Kalam had these precious gifts meticulously photographed and catalogued. A ritual to acknowledge the respect and goodwill they represented. But here lies the essence of his character—he never gazed upon them again. No lingering attachment, no desire for earthly possessions could tether him.

When he left Rashtrapathi Bhavan, he did not even take away a pencil from the gifts he had received. Here was a man who was detached from material goods and earthly desires. In a world often swayed by materialism, he stood firm, teaching us that true greatness lies in detachment, in rising above the allure of fleeting treasures.

***

In the archives of history, Dr. Kalam's detachment echoes loudly— a reminder that true greatness is found not in what we accumulate, but in what we give, and leave behind for the greater good. When you become detached mentally from yourself and concentrate on helping other people with their difficulties, you will be able to cope with your own problems more effectively. Sri Chinmoy said, "Your heart must become a sea of love. Your mind must become a river of detachment."

20. THE LIGHT IN ADVERSITY

"Our greatest glory is not in never falling, but in rising every time we fall." – Confucius

In the chill of a December night in 1914, West Orange, New Jersey, bore witness to a tragedy that would have shattered most spirits. Thomas Edison's supposedly fireproof factory erupted in flames, casting an eerie glow against the dark sky. The inventor's dreams, painstakingly forged within the concrete and steel walls, seemed to crumble in the inferno.

As the blaze roared, Edison's son, Charles, frantically sought his father amidst the chaos. Finally locating him, he found Thomas Edison standing stoically, his white hair billowing in the wind, face illuminated by the destructive beauty of the flames. The 67-year-old inventor, witnessing a lifetime's work vanish, displayed an unexpected resilience.

"My heart ached for him," Charles recalled. Yet, in that moment of profound loss, Edison's response was a testament to an extraordinary mindset. "Find your mother! Bring her here! She'll never see anything like this as long as she lives," Edison exclaimed. His focus was not on despair but on sharing a profound experience.

The morning after, facing the ruins of his life's work, Edison uttered words that echoed the resilience of a true visionary. "There's value in disaster, all our mistakes are burned up. Thank God, we can start anew." In the ashes of destruction, Edison found the seed of renewal, embodying the indomitable spirit that turns adversity into opportunity.

***

Like Edison, let us see the value in disaster, for it is in the ruins of our mistakes that we find the fertile ground to build anew and rise, stronger than before. Edison's story teaches us that within the ashes of failure and loss lies the potential for rebirth. Embrace setbacks as stepping stones, for in the face of disaster, the resilient spirit finds the strength to start anew.

21. THE DESTRUCTIVE POWER OF ASSUMPTIONS

"Your assumptions are your windows on the world. Scrub them off every once in a while, or the light won't come in." – Isaac Asimov

In the bustling confines of the airport lounge, a weary business traveller sought solace in a book, a cup of coffee, and a small packet of gingernut biscuits. Little did she know that this ordinary moment would unfold into a tale of assumptions and unexpected twists.

Seated beside a stranger, engrossed in her reading, she absentmindedly reached for a biscuit. To her astonishment, the stranger casually took one too, indulging without a word. Shocked but silent, she continued reading, nervously consuming a third biscuit, only to witness the stranger take the fourth with the same nonchalance.

As if the universe enjoyed a sense of irony, the stranger extended the packet, offering her the last biscuit. Unable to contain her indignation, the lady gathered her belongings, shot the stranger a scowl, and marched off to the boarding gate.

However, the punchline awaited her at the gate. Upon reaching for her boarding ticket, she discovered her unopened, untouched packet of gingernuts. The stranger's calm sharing wasn't an act of audacity but a simple, genuine gesture.

***

In the unopened packets of life, our assumptions often rob us of shared moments. Before jumping to conclusions, let's savour the richness of understanding that comes from breaking the biscuit of assumption. According to research conducted by Harvard, 70% of all our assumptions are wrong. In a world where quick judgements can lead to misunderstandings, it's crucial to pause, communicate, and not let appearances deceive us.

22. FOCUS ON THE SOLUTION, NOT THE PROBLEM

"Always turn a negative situation into a positive situation." –Michael Jordan

In the confined shadows of a prison cell, a young man faced an unjust sentence for a crime he hadn't committed. Meanwhile, his ageing father, living on a farm, grappled with the weight of unyielding fields and a body weakened by time. A heartfelt letter bridged the distance between them.

"Son, this year I'm unable to plant anything. My strength has left me, and I can't dig the ground. I know if you were here, you would have helped me," the father expressed in a plea for assistance. The son, confined but resourceful, responded with a letter that would unknowingly sow the seeds of liberation.

In a cunning move to divert suspicion, the son wrote, "Dad, please do not dig the land. I've hidden guns in different places on the ground. It's dangerous!" The prison manager, unaware of the son's true intentions, promptly handed the letter to the police.

A team of officers descended upon the farm, fervently digging up the Earth in search of hidden firearms. Yet, the soil yielded no weapons. In a twist of poetic justice, the son, in his next letter, offered solace to his father. "Dad, now that the ground has been dug up, you can plant your vegetables. I did the best I could do from here. I love you!"

Touched by the sincerity of the son's sacrifice, the police, realising the innocence of the imprisoned youth, released him without charges. Joy and relief embraced the father as his son returned home, the fields ready for cultivation, and the bonds of love triumphant over injustice.

***

In the garden of adversity, the seeds of love and sacrifice often bloom into the flowers of freedom and redemption. Life is full of problems, uncertainties, and issues, and we need to cope with these situations innovatively. Examples include injustices, unjust punishments, managing one's relationships so that they are healthy and functional, surviving disabilities, coping with grief, loss, and self-esteem issues. If you are strong-willed, determined, and creative, you can find a way out, even if the condition is not favourable.

23. QUILLS OF UNITY

"No relationship is all sunshine, but 2 people can share one umbrella and survive the storm together."
– Unknown

In the grip of the coldest winter, a community of porcupines faced a dire choice—unite and endure the freezing cold, or distance themselves and succumb to isolation. The bitter reality of their quills causing harm in their attempt to share warmth forced them to reconsider their approach.

Initially, they chose solitude, a seemingly safer path. Yet, as the icy winds of isolation swept through, the porcupines found themselves succumbing to the harshness of the winter. Alone and frozen, they realised the cost of distancing was far greater than the wounds inflicted by their closest companions.

Faced with a crucial decision, the porcupines opted for unity. They embraced the truth that close relationships, while not devoid of challenges, offered a warmth that surpassed the sting of minor wounds. Learning to live with the imperfections of their close bond, they discovered a strength that transcended the bitter chill around them.

In the end, the porcupines survived the coldest winter ever. Their quills, once a source of pain, became a symbol of resilience and the enduring power of unity. They taught us that in the face of life's harshest storms, the warmth of companionship is a force that can conquer even the most frigid challenges.

***

In the dance of unity, we may bear the quills of imperfections, but it is through the warmth of connection that we survive the coldest winters of life. The story of the porcupines reminds us that the warmth of connection and unity often outweighs the small wounds that may arise in close relationships. In the coldest of times, it is our shared warmth that sustains us.

24. WINGS OF RENEWAL

"Only I can change my life. No one can do it for me."
– Carol Burnett

In the vast expanse of nature, the eagle stands as a symbol of resilience and rebirth. The majestic bird, blessed with the longest lifespan of its species, embarks on a remarkable journey of transformation to achieve its extraordinary longevity.

As the eagle reaches its 40s, the challenges of ageing become apparent. Its once formidable talons lose their grip, the sharp beak becomes bent, and the once soaring wings become burdened by thick, heavy feathers. Faced with the inevitability of decline, the eagle confronts a pivotal choice: succumb to the limitations of age or embrace a painful process of change.

Choosing the path of renewal, the eagle ascends to a mountaintop, finding solace on its nest. There, against the unyielding resistance of a rock, the eagle bravely plucks out its worn beak—a symbolic act of shedding the past to make room for the future. Patiently, it awaits the growth of a new beak—a symbol of adaptation and renewal.

The process continues as the eagle, now equipped with a new beak, turns to its talons, tearing away the old and embracing the promise of regeneration. With renewed strength and purpose, it proceeds to pluck out its old-aged feathers, shedding the weight of the past. After 150 days—a metaphorical gestation period—the eagle takes its famous flight of rebirth.

This majestic journey concludes with the eagle soaring through the skies for another 30 years, a living testament to the power of embracing change and undergoing transformation to overcome the challenges of time.

***

Like the eagle, may we find the courage to pluck away the old, and with renewed wings, take flight into the vast expanse of our own rebirth, embracing the beauty of change. The eagle's tale teaches us that in the face of ageing and adversity, the willingness to undergo painful but necessary change leads to a soaring rebirth. Embrace transformation, for it is the key to a prolonged and fulfilled life.

25. BE TRUE TO CHARACTER

"Good character is not formed in a week or a month. It is created little by little, day by day. Protracted and patient effort is needed to develop good character. A man's character is his guardian divinity." – Heraclitus

A mother once brought her child to Mahatma Gandhi and asked him to tell the young boy to stop eating sugar because it was not good for his diet or his developing teeth. Gandhi replied, "I am sorry. I cannot tell him that now. Maybe you can bring him back in a month." Gandhi then moved on, brushing aside the mother's request. She was upset; she had travelled some distance and had expected the mighty leader to support her parenting effort. But having little recourse, she left for her home. One month later, however, she returned, not knowing what to expect.

The great Gandhi took the small child's hands into his own, knelt before him, and tenderly said, "Do not eat sugar, my child. It is not good for you." Then Gandhi embraced the boy and returned him to his mother. Grateful but perplexed, the mother queried, "Why didn't you say that a month ago?" "Well," said Gandhi, "a month ago, I myself was addicted to sugar."

***

One of the greatest assets a person can have is self-discipline and strength of character based on universal principles. However, a strong character is not easily acquired. It is developed over time as we are tested and our values and judgement skills are refined and tempered. People who have a strong character withstand tests and temptations by holding true to time-honoured principles that have been identified as being good and honourable throughout the course of human history.

26. KNOW YOUR PURPOSE IN LIFE

"It's not enough to have lived. We should be determined to live for something." – Winston S. Churchill

In the quiet workshop of the Pencil Maker, a conversation unfolded between creator and creation, revealing profound lessons that transcended the realm of simple writing utensils. The Pencil Maker imparted 5 essential truths to the pencil, a guide to becoming the best version of itself. First, it was reminded, "You will be able to do many great things, but only if you allow yourself to be held in someone's hand." A poignant reminder that true purpose is realised when surrendered to a greater force.

The second lesson spoke of inevitable challenges: "You will experience a painful sharpening from time to time, but this is required if you are to become a better pencil." Growth often comes through adversity, and the pencil, like us, must endure moments of discomfort to refine its essence.

The third lesson granted the power of redemption: "You have the ability to correct any mistakes you might make." Mistakes are not the end but an opportunity for improvement—a chance to rewrite the narrative.

The fourth lesson delved into the essence of character: "The most important part of you will always be what's inside." Beyond the outer facade, true worth lies within, emphasising the importance of integrity and substance.

Lastly, the pencil was charged with a significant responsibility: "You are expected to leave a mark. No matter what the condition, you must continue to write. You must always leave a clear, legible mark no matter how difficult the situation." Even in adversity, the pencil must persist, leaving a mark that transcends challenges.

The pencil, understanding its purpose, embraced these profound teachings and entered the pencil box with a solemn promise to remember its calling—a reminder for us all to carry the wisdom of the Pencil Maker in our hearts.

***

The lessons from the Pencil Maker resonate with the essence of our own journey. Surrender, resilience, redemption, character, and leaving a meaningful mark define a purposeful existence. Like the pencil, may we embrace the wisdom of life's lessons: to surrender to a greater force, endure challenges for growth, correct our mistakes, cherish our inner worth, and persist in leaving a meaningful mark in the world.

27. THE WONDERS WITHIN

"The best and most beautiful things in the world cannot be seen or even touched – they must be felt with the heart." – Helen Keller

In a classroom discussion about the "Seven Wonders of the World," a group of American school children offered their perspectives on iconic structures and marvels. As the votes were collected, the teacher noticed one student who hadn't completed her list.

Curious, the teacher approached the girl, asking if she needed help. The little girl hesitated before sharing her unique perspective, "I couldn't quite make up my mind because there were so many." Encouraged to share, the girl unfolded a list that resonated with profound simplicity.

Her list read: 1. To see; 2. To hear; 3. To touch; 4. To taste; 5. To feel; 6. To laugh; and 7. To love. The room, once abuzz with discussion, fell silent, captivated by the unexpected beauty of the child's perspective. The essence of life's wonders distilled into moments of profound human experience.

As the child concluded her list, a wave of applause erupted. The entire class, moved by the profound wisdom of a child, stood up to cheer. In that moment, the little girl's list became a reminder that the most extraordinary wonders are not always external marvels but the simple, yet profound, experiences that shape our humanity.

***

The story highlights the beauty of simplicity and the profound wonders found in the fabric of everyday life. Sometimes, the most extraordinary wonders are the ones that touch our hearts. In the quiet wisdom of a child's list, we rediscover that the true wonders of the world are the moments that stir our senses, bring joy to our hearts, and connect us through the threads of laughter and love.

28. UNWAVERING LOVE

"True love is selfless. It is prepared to sacrifice." – Sadhu Vaswani

On a bustling morning around 8:30 am, an elderly gentleman in his 80s arrived at the clinic, seeking to have stitches removed from his thumb. Despite the evident urgency, he mentioned having an appointment at 9:30 am, hinting at a deeper commitment.

Curious, the caregiver engaged in conversation, discovering that the man's rush was fuelled by a heartfelt dedication. When asked about his impending appointment, he revealed, "I need to go to the nursing home to have breakfast with my wife." The nurse, empathetic, inquired about her health, and the elderly man shared that his wife had been battling Alzheimer's Disease for a while.

In the midst of tending to his wound, the caregiver couldn't help but express concern about potential delays. To this, the elderly gentleman calmly responded, "She no longer knows who I am and hasn't recognised me in 5 years." Surprised, the caregiver probed further, "And you still go every morning, even though she doesn't know who you are?"

With a gentle smile and a pat on the hand, the man imparted a profound truth, "She doesn't know me, but I still know who she is. So, I must."

In those simple words, the elderly gentleman encapsulated the enduring power of love and commitment.

Despite the heart-wrenching reality of his wife's fading recognition, he continued to show up every morning, honouring a connection that transcended the limitations of memory.

***

The poignant story reminds us that love, in its purest form, goes beyond the bounds of recognition. In the face of Alzheimer's, the elderly gentleman's daily visits embody a profound commitment to the enduring essence of a shared life. In the quiet dedication of a daily breakfast, we witness a love that withstands the erosion of memory. A reminder that true commitment transcends the boundaries of time and recognition.

29. THE PRICE OF HANDS

"All that I am or hope to be I owe to my angel mother."
– Abraham Lincoln

A young and promising candidate applied for a managerial position in a prestigious company. His academic prowess shone through, leading to successful interviews. The director, intrigued by the youth's achievements, asked about scholarships and financial support. The youth revealed that his mother, a clothes cleaner, single-handedly financed his education since his father's passing at one year old.

Curious, the director asked to see the youth's hands. To his surprise, they were smooth and unblemished. Inquiring about the youth's involvement in washing clothes, the response was a candid acknowledgement that his mother insisted he prioritise studying, as she could wash clothes faster than him.

The director issued a request: "When you go back home today, clean your mother's hands, and then come and see me." The youth, feeling a mix of emotions, followed the director's advice. As he gently washed his mother's hands, tears rolled down his cheeks, realising for the first time the sacrifices behind his education.

The next morning, the youth visited the director and proudly declared, "Sir, I washed my mother's hands and finished washing all the remaining clothes." In that moment, the director recognised the qualities he sought in a manager—empathy, humility, and a deep appreciation for the sacrifices made for one's success.

The youth's appointment symbolised more than a professional achievement; it represented a recognition of the unseen hands that toiled to pave the way for a brighter future.

***

This poignant story serves as a reminder that success often comes with a price, and acknowledging the sacrifices of those who paved the way is crucial. True leadership encompasses empathy and an understanding of the human stories behind the achievements. In the quiet moments of recognising our roots, we find the strength to lead with empathy and gratitude. Success is not just personal; it's a reflection of the hands that shaped our journey.

30. LOVE BEYOND SIGHT

"The only thing that you can never have too much of is love." — Brian Tracy

A man married a beautiful girl. He loved her very much. One day she developed a skin disease. Slowly she started to lose her beauty. It so happened that one day her husband left for a tour. While returning, he met with an accident and lost his eyesight. However, their married life continued as usual. But as days passed, she lost her beauty gradually. The blind husband did not know this, and there was not any difference in their love for each other. He continued to love her, and she also loved him very much. One day she died. Her death brought him great sorrow. He finished all her last rites and wanted to leave that town.

A man from behind called and said, "Now how will you be able to walk all alone? All these days your wife used to help you". He replied, "I am not blind. I was acting because if she knew I could see her skin condition due to a disease, it would have pained her more than her disease. I didn't love her for her beauty alone, but I fell in love with her caring and loving nature. So, I pretended to be blind. I only wanted to keep her happy".

***

When you truly love someone, you will go to any extent to keep your loved one happy. Sometimes it is good for us to act blind and ignore one another's shortcomings in order to be happy. Beauty will fade with time, but the heart and soul will always be the same. Love the person for what he/she is from inside, not from the outside.

31. THE TRIPLE FILTER TEST

"Those who gossip evil things about others should remember that no one is perfect, including themselves."
– Terry Mark

One day, a curious disciple approached the great Greek Philosopher Socrates, eager to share some information about his friend. Before allowing the conversation to proceed, Socrates interjected, "Just a minute. Before you tell me anything about my friend, I'd like you to pass the Triple Filter Test."

Perplexed, the disciple inquired about the test, and Socrates explained. "The first filter is the filter of Truth. Have you made absolutely sure that what you are about to tell me is true?" The disciple nodded, prompting Socrates to delve into the second filter, "The filter of Goodness. Is what you are about to tell me about my friend something good?" Again, the disciple affirmed.

Socrates continued with the third filter, "The filter of Usefulness. Is what you are about to tell me about my friend going to be useful to me?" At this point, the disciple hesitated, confessing, "Sorry, I cannot pass any of the 3 tests."

Socrates, ever the wise philosopher, concluded with a timeless lesson, "Well, if what you want to tell me is neither true, good, nor even useful, why tell me at all?"

In this simple yet profound exchange, Socrates imparts the importance of mindful communication—encouraging truthfulness, goodness, and usefulness in the information we choose to share with others.

***

The Triple Filter Test serves as a reminder that the words we choose to convey should be grounded in truth, goodness, and usefulness. A thoughtful approach to communication can foster understanding and harmony. Before you speak, run your words through the filters of truth, goodness, and usefulness. In doing so, you contribute to a world where words carry meaning and purpose.

32. SAVING POWER OF PRAYER

"God answers prayers, but he doesn't always answer it your way." – Lou Holtz

Irmgard Wood, a young girl in Germany during World War II, shares a poignant story that transcends borders and illustrates the power of compassion and prayer. One morning, as she and her family witnessed an American plane being hit and falling in flames from the sky, her mother, despite the enmity of war, instinctively whispered a prayer for the pilot.

Years later, the family found themselves in America after immigrating. Irmgard's mother secured a job in a California hospital. In a twist of fate, one day, a patient, learning of her German background, inquired about her hometown in Germany. When she mentioned Stuttgart, the patient recounted a miraculous escape over Stuttgart during the war. His plane had been hit, and he had fallen from the sky in flames.

Emotionally, the patient shared, "I got out on time, and I just don't know how I did it because I can never remember the details. To this day, I am convinced that there was somebody praying for me."

In this heartwarming tale, the lines between friend and foe blur as prayers offered in the midst of conflict echo across time and space, reminding us of the profound impact of compassion and the universal desire for peace.

***

The story underscores the transformative power of prayer and compassion, transcending divisions created by war. It serves as a reminder that, in the face of adversity, the shared humanity in us all can bridge even the widest gaps. In the echoes of a whispered prayer, the boundaries of war dissolve, revealing the universal language of compassion that unites us all as one human family.

33. DR. KALAM'S SILENT CHARITY

"I will work and sweat for a great vision, the vision of transforming India into a developed nation."
– APJ Abdul Kalam

In 2002, when Dr. APJ Abdul Kalam assumed the presidency in India, the month of Ramadan coincided with July-August. Traditionally, the President hosted an Iftar party during this period. However, Dr. Kalam, known for his simplicity and commitment to social causes, questioned the necessity of hosting a lavish party for those who were already, well-fed.

Upon learning that the Iftar party would cost around Rs. 22 lakhs, Dr. Kalam made a remarkable decision. He directed Mr. Nair, his secretary, to donate that amount to selected orphanages in the form of food, dresses, and blankets. The responsibility of selecting the orphanages was delegated to a team in Rashtrapathi Bhavan, and Dr. Kalam played no role in the selection process.

After the selection was completed, Dr. Kalam called Mr. Nair into his room and handed him a personal cheque for Rs. 1 lakh. He explained that this amount was a contribution from his personal savings and requested that it remain confidential.

Mr. Nair, astonished by this gesture, suggested sharing the information publicly to showcase Dr. Kalam's selfless act. Dr. Kalam, however, insisted on keeping it discreet, embodying the essence of silent charity. Dr. Kalam's actions speak louder than words, revealing a leader who not only refrained from ostentatious celebrations but also quietly extended his personal resources to make a positive impact on the lives of those in need.

***

"Dr. Kalam's Silent Charity" exemplifies the depth of compassion and humility in leadership. It serves as a reminder that genuine acts of kindness often occur behind closed doors, driven by a sincere commitment to making a difference. In the quiet corridors of compassion, Dr. Kalam's silent charity echoes a profound truth—leadership is not just about power but about the silent, selfless acts that uplift the vulnerable and embody the spirit of service.

34. THE COST OF DISTRACTION

"It's not enough to be busy; so are the ants. The question is: what are we busy about?" – Henry David Thoreau

In a coastal zone, a diligent guard was entrusted with the crucial responsibility of maintaining a lighthouse along a perilous coast. The primary task was simple yet paramount: to keep the lamp burning every night for the safety of passing ships.

The guard, however, found his compassion tested when people approached him with various needs. A desperate woman sought oil to keep her child warm, a farmer requested some for his son's studies, and another man needed it for his engine. Driven by kindness, the guard shared the limited oil he had, neglecting the core duty of the lighthouse.

As the month progressed, the inevitable consequence unfolded. With no oil left for the lighthouse lamp, a tragic night ensued. Three ships were wrecked, and a hundred lives were lost in the darkness.

When confronted, the guard offered seemingly valid excuses, justifying his actions. However, the prosecutor's words cut deep: "You were given only one task—to keep the lamp burning in the lighthouse. Everything else was secondary. Your failure caused the shipwreck and the loss of a hundred lives."

***

"The Cost of Distraction" underscores the importance of prioritising core responsibilities. It serves as a powerful lesson about the impact of well-intentioned but misguided actions on the greater good. In the realm of responsibilities, let the core task be the guiding light, for distractions, no matter how noble, may lead to unforeseen darkness and consequences.

35. SELF ASSESSMENT

"Every job is a self-portrait of the person who did it. Autograph your work with excellence." – Jessica Guidobono

In a small town, a curious little boy found himself at a telephone booth near a store's cash counter. Dialling a number, he engaged in a conversation that caught the attention of the store owner, who observed the interaction:

Boy: "Madam, can you give me the job of cutting your lawn?" Woman: "I already have someone to cut my lawn." Boy: "Madam, I will cut your lawn for half the price that the person who cuts your lawn charges." Woman: "I'm very satisfied with the person who is presently cutting my lawn." Boy: "Madam, I'll even sweep the floor and the stairs of your house for free." Woman: "No, thank you."

With a smile on his face, the little boy replaced the receiver. Intrigued, the store owner approached him and said, "Son, I like your attitude, and I would like to offer you a job."

The boy, with surprising confidence, declined, saying, "No thanks."

Perplexed, the store owner questioned, "But you were really pleading for one."

The boy replied, "No sir, I was just monitoring my own performance at the job I already have. I am the one who is working for that lady I was talking to!"

***

The story highlights the value of self-assessment and taking ownership of one's efforts, even at a young age. Self-appraisal is an important part of the performance appraisal process where the employee himself gets feedback on his performance. Do you ever check on your own life and performance? Have you been achieving the dreams and aspirations that you have outlined in your life? How happy are you with your life, the way you experience it?

36. SUCCESS DOES NOT HAPPEN IN ISOLATION

"Giving is not about making a donation; it's about making a difference." – Kathy Calvin

In the heart of a rural community, there lived a farmer renowned for cultivating superior, award-winning corn. Year after year, he proudly entered his corn in the state competition, consistently earning honours and prizes.

One day, a curious newspaper reporter sought an interview with the accomplished farmer, hoping to unveil the secrets behind his success. During the conversation, the reporter made a fascinating discovery about the farmer's approach to farming.

The farmer revealed a practice that set him apart—he generously shared his best seeds with his neighbours. Perplexed, the reporter questioned, "How can you afford to share your best seed with your neighbours, especially when they too participate in the corn fair each year alongside you? Don't you worry about the competition?"

With a wise and knowing smile, the farmer responded, "Don't you know? The wind picks up pollen from the ripening corn and swirls it from field to field. If my neighbours grow inferior, sub-standard, and poor-quality corn, cross-pollination will steadily degrade the quality of my own corn. If I am to grow good corn, I must help my neighbours to grow good corn as well."

***

The story teaches us that success is not solely an individual pursuit but a collective endeavour. By uplifting those around us, we contribute to shared prosperity that benefits everyone. In the vast fields of life, the seeds of success flourish not in isolation but in the fertile soil of collaboration, where each individual's growth contributes to the collective abundance.

37. THE MIRROR OF SELF REFLECTION

"Either push your limits or suffocate in your comfort zone." – Arun Purang

One day, as the employees entered the office, they were met with a surprising message on the door: "Yesterday, the person who has been hindering your growth in this company passed away. We invite you to join the funeral that has been prepared in the conference hall."

Initially, a wave of sadness swept through the office as they mourned the loss of a colleague. However, as time passed, curiosity replaced grief. The employees began wondering who this mysterious person was, the one supposedly impeding their progress. As they approached the conference hall for the funeral, the atmosphere buzzed with anticipation.

As the employees neared the coffin, the excitement reached its peak. Each person eagerly sought to unveil the identity of the individual who had hindered their growth. However, what they found inside left them speechless and contemplative. A mirror adorned the interior of the coffin, reflecting their own images back at them. A sign beside the mirror carried a powerful message: "There is only one person who is capable of setting limits to your growth, and that is YOU."

The employees were confronted with a profound truth—the barriers to their own progress were not external forces but their own perceptions, actions, and limitations.

***

"The Mirror of Self-Reflection" urges us to recognise that our greatest obstacles often lie within ourselves. By embracing self-awareness and taking responsibility for our growth, we unlock the true potential that resides within. In the journey of self-discovery, the mirror of self-reflection reveals the power to break free from self-imposed limitations and pave the way for boundless growth and success.

38. THE BEAUTY IN IMPERFECTION

"Imperfection is beauty, madness is genius, and it's better to be absolutely ridiculous than absolutely boring." – Marilyn Monroe

In ancient China, there lived a humble water bearer who owned 2 large pots. Each pot hung on either end of a pole, which he carried across his neck. One pot was perfectly intact, always delivering a full portion of water. The other, however, had a noticeable crack and only managed to arrive half-full at the end of the bearer's long journey from the stream to his house.

For 2 years, this routine continued. The perfect pot swelled with pride at its flawless performance, while the cracked pot wallowed in shame and sadness, feeling inadequate due to its inability to fulfil its purpose completely. One day, consumed by its perceived failure, the cracked pot spoke to the water bearer. "I am ashamed," it lamented, "for my flaw causes me to leak water, failing to deliver a full portion."

The bearer, with a gentle smile, responded, "Have you noticed the flowers blooming only on your side of the path, but not on the other pot's side? I have always known about your flaws and planted flower seeds there. Each day, as we walked back, you watered them. For 2 years, your unique trait has allowed me to pick these beautiful flowers to decorate our home. Without you, just as you are, this beauty would not exist."

***

Embrace your imperfections, for they may lead to unexpected beauty and purpose. Like the cracked pot, what we perceive as flaws can actually be sources of unique strength and contribution. In our differences lies our ability to bring unmatched beauty into the world, showing that perfection lies not in flawlessness, but in embracing and utilising our unique characteristics.

39. LESSONS AT THE DINNER TABLE

"Age is an issue of mind over matter. If you don't mind, it doesn't matter." – Mark Twain

In a humble household, an elderly grandfather, with trembling hands and blurred vision, struggled to eat without making a mess. His son and daughter-in-law, irritated by the spilled milk and scattered food, decided to isolate him at a small table in the corner, serving his meals in a wooden bowl to avoid further breakages.

The grandfather ate his meals in silence, often with tears in his eyes, as the rest of the family enjoyed their dinner without him. His presence became merely a source of sharp admonitions for any minor mishaps.

Amidst this, the four-year-old grandson was quietly observing everything. One evening, the father found his son playing with a piece of wood. Curiously, he asked what the boy was making. "A little bowl," the child replied innocently, "for you and Mama to eat from when you're as old as Grandpa."

These words struck the parents profoundly. In a moment of profound realisation, tears welled up in their eyes. That very evening, the father took his elderly father's hand and led him back to the family table. From that day on, the grandfather ate every meal with the family. The dropped forks and spilled milk no longer seemed to bother anyone. The son's simple, yet profound act of empathy and understanding reminded the family of the importance of compassion, respect, and the cherished value of family.

***

Empathy has the power to transform perspectives and heal divisions. The wisdom of a child reminds us that kindness and respect towards our elders is a reflection of our humanity. In caring for those who once cared for us, we learn the true essence of family, love, and compassion.

40. THE PRICE OF SHORTCUTS

"In the end, we only regret the chances we didn't take, relationships we were afraid to have, and the decisions we waited too long to make." – Lewis Carroll

In a serene forest, there sang a lark, its melodies a symbol of freedom and joy. One day, a man with a box full of worms walked through the forest. Curious, the lark halted his song to inquire about the contents of the box. The man explained he was heading to the market to trade the worms for feathers.

Seizing an opportunity, the lark proposed a trade: its feathers for the man's worms. This exchange would save the lark the effort of hunting for food. The man agreed, and the lark gave up a feather for a meal. This arrangement continued day after day.

However, with each passing day, the lark gave away more of its feathers. Initially, it seemed a fair trade, but as time went on, the consequences of its choices became apparent. The day came when the lark had no feathers left. It could no longer fly or hunt for food. The once beautiful and melodious bird, now bare and grounded, lost its essence and soon, its life.

***

This lark, once a symbol of freedom and joy, had sacrificed its very nature for the sake of convenience. The shortcuts it took for temporary ease led to its ultimate downfall, a poignant reminder of the price of prioritising immediate gratification over long-term well-being. Shortcuts may seem appealing, but they often come at a great cost. Like the lark trading its feathers for worms, we must be cautious not to sacrifice our essential qualities for temporary gains. True strength lies in facing challenges, not avoiding them. Remember, the choices we make today shape our tomorrow.

41. THE REFORMED THIEF: A JOURNEY TO SAINTHOOD

"We are all called to be holy by living our lives with love and by bearing witness in everything we do, wherever we find ourselves." – Pope Francis

In the early days of history, when punishments were harsh, a man caught stealing a sheep faced severe consequences. The authorities branded his forehead with a red-hot iron, marking him with the initials 'ST' for 'Sheep Thief.' This scar was to be a lifelong reminder of his crime, an indelible mark of shame.

However, this man, marked by his past, embarked on a transformative journey. He began to reform his life, making amends for his mistake. His transformation was profound; he became a role model in his village, known for his good behaviour and charitable works. He dedicated his life to service and kindness, reshaping not only his identity but also the perception of those around him.

Years passed, and the man grew old, yet the letters 'ST' remained visible on his wrinkled forehead. But the meaning these letters held for the villagers had changed dramatically. When children asked about the 'ST', their parents would smile and respond, "It stands for 'Saint'."

As the man's life drew to a close, the entire village gathered to be by his side. They prayed to him, for in their eyes, he was indeed a saint. This man once branded a thief had not only redeemed himself but had also become a symbol of hope and transformation.

***

True redemption lies in our actions and the ability to transform our lives. Like the man branded as a thief who became a saint, we too can redefine our identity through positive deeds and love. His story teaches us that with faith, determination, and the courage to change, we can overcome our past and inspire others.

42. UNITY IN DIVERSITY: THE LESSON OF ABDUL KALAM

"Unity in diversity is India's strength. There is simplicity in every Indian. There is unity in every corner of India. This is our strength." – Abdul Kalam

In a small village school, 2 best friends, Abdul Kalam and Ramanadha Sastry, shared a bench in their classroom. Abdul, a Muslim, and Ramanadha, a Hindu Brahmin and the son of the head priest, embodied the harmonious blend of diverse cultures. Their friendship was a testament to the unity that transcended religious boundaries.

However, this harmony was challenged when a new teacher arrived. He objected to Abdul, a Muslim boy, sitting beside a Hindu Brahmin. In a tone laced with prejudice, he instructed Abdul to move to the last bench. This act of discrimination deeply hurt both boys, symbolising a rift in the unity they had always known.

The head priest, upon learning about this incident, took immediate and strong action. He summoned the teacher and expressed his disapproval of such divisive behaviour in an educational setting. The priest emphasised that the role of a teacher was to foster religious harmony and understanding, not to seed young minds with biases based on superficial differences.

Realising his mistake, the teacher sought Abdul Kalam's forgiveness. His remorse was sincere, and acknowledging this, the head priest allowed him to continue his teaching role. This incident became a pivotal lesson for the entire school community, reinforcing the importance of respect, understanding, and unity amidst diversity.

***

True education lies in learning to respect and embrace diversity. Abdul Kalam's story teaches us that our strength lies in our unity, not in our differences. When we look beyond superficial distinctions and value each person's unique identity, we foster a world of harmony and understanding. Let's remember to cherish diversity as our greatest teacher.

43. A NEW WORLD THROUGH NEW EYES

"The only thing worse than being blind is having sight but no vision." – Helen Keller

On a train journey, a father and his 25-year-old son, newly sighted, sat side by side. The son, with the wide-eyed wonder of a child, gazed out the window in amazement. "Dad, look at those tall trees! They're moving along with us!" he exclaimed with joy. His father, smiling warmly, shared in his son's newfound discovery of the world.

Nearby, 2 women observed the young man's exclamations with curiosity and then pity, assuming his behaviour was unusual. When the son expressed his delight again, "Dad, look at those clouds! They're pink and white, and they're running too!" the women couldn't help but express their sympathy to the father. "I'm sorry about your son. Have you taken him to see a doctor?" one of them asked.

The father's response was gentle yet revealing. "I did, Madam. We are just coming from the hospital in the Capital. My son was blind from birth; he just got his eyes today." This revelation transformed the women's pity into awe and understanding. They realised that they were witnessing a beautiful moment of a young man seeing the world for the first time.

The son's innocent wonder and the father's quiet pride painted a vivid picture of gratitude, joy, and the beauty of experiencing the world anew. This journey was not just a physical one but a journey into a world of sight, full of colours, shapes, and movements, a world that the son was seeing for the very first time.

***

Life's most beautiful moments often come from new perspectives. The story of the son gaining his sight reminds us to appreciate the wonder around us, often-overlooked in our familiarity. It teaches us to view the world through the lens of gratitude and marvel at everyday miracles. Let's cherish and celebrate each new experience, as each one offers a unique and precious perspective on the world.

44. THE MEXICAN FISHERMAN

"Contentment is natural wealth; luxury is artificial poverty." – Socrates

In a small coastal Mexican village, an American businessman witnessed a fisherman docking his boat with a catch of large yellowfin tuna. Impressed, he asked how long it took to catch them. The fisherman casually replied, "Only a little while."

Curious, the businessman suggested he stay out longer to catch more fish. The fisherman explained he had enough to support his family and live a carefree life. Intrigued, the businessman inquired about his leisure time. The fisherman described a simple, fulfilling life: sleeping early, fishing a bit, playing with his children, taking siestas with his wife, and enjoying evenings with friends in the village.

The businessman, who was formerly a university professor, saw an opportunity. He outlined a business plan for the fisherman: spend more time fishing, buy a bigger boat, expand to a fleet, sell directly to consumers, open a canning factory, and eventually move to larger cities to manage the growing enterprise. In 15-20 years, he could launch an IPO, become rich, and retire to a small coastal village to enjoy life.

"Sir, I'm already in a small coastal village, enjoying my life," said the fisherman.

***

Embrace the wisdom of the Mexican fisherman. Wealth isn't measured in possessions but in life's simple joys and moments of peace. Like him, recognise the richness in your present life. Don't chase distant dreams at the expense of today's happiness. Remember, the greatest treasure is often found not in future achievements but in cherishing the here and now. Live fully, love deeply, and find joy in life's simple pleasures.

45. FOOTPRINTS IN THE SAND

"Faith is taking the first step even when you don't see the whole staircase." – Martin Luther King Jr.

One night, a man dreamed he was walking along a beach with the Lord. The sky above them was a canvas, displaying scenes from his life. As he observed each scene, he noticed 2 sets of footprints in the sand, one belonging to him and the other to the Lord.

However, as the last scene of his life flashed before him, he looked back at the footprints and was perplexed. During many instances, particularly at the lowest and saddest times of his life, there was only one set of footprints. This observation troubled him deeply.

Confused and somewhat troubled, he questioned the Lord. "Lord, you promised that once I decided to follow you, you would walk with me all the way. But I have noticed that during the most troublesome times in my life, there is only one set of footprints. I don't understand why, when I needed you most, you would leave me."

The Lord's reply was tender and comforting. "My son, my precious child, I love you, and I would never leave you. During your times of trial and suffering, when you see only one set of footprints, it was then that I was carrying you."

***

In our darkest hours, when we feel most alone, it is then that we are carried by a greater force. The man understood that during his most challenging times, when he felt most alone, it was actually the Lord who bore him through his difficulties, carrying him when he lacked the strength to walk on his own. The dream was a poignant reminder of the Lord's constant presence and unwavering support, even in the most trying times. In faith, we find the strength to endure and the assurance that we are never truly alone.

46. SANDS OF FORGIVENESS AND STONES OF GRATITUDE

"Gratitude is the fairest blossom which springs from the soul." – Henry Ward Beecher

In a vast desert, 2 friends, Paul and Jeffrey, embarked on a journey. Amid their travel, a heated argument ensued, and in a moment of anger, Jeffrey slapped Paul. The sting of the slap was sharp, but Paul's reaction was unexpected. He simply bent down and wrote in the sand, "Today, my best friend slapped me in the face." Then, without a word, they continued their journey.

Soon, they stumbled upon an oasis and decided to bathe in its waters. However, as Paul was bathing, he found himself trapped in the mire, struggling for breath, on the verge of drowning. Jeffrey, without a second thought, leaped in to rescue his friend. Paul's life was saved by the very hands that had hurt him earlier.

After recovering from this near-fatal experience, Paul did something remarkable. He carved a message on a stone: "Today, my best friend saved my life." Jeffrey, puzzled by these contrasting responses, asked Paul why he chose to write in the sand earlier and now on a stone.

Paul's reply was profound, "When someone hurts us, we should write it down in sand, where the winds of forgiveness can erase it. But when someone does something good for us, we must engrave it in stone, where no wind can ever erase it."

***

Forgiveness and gratitude are the cornerstones of lasting relationships. The story of Paul and Jeffrey teaches us to let go of hurt, like words in the sand, easily washed away by the winds of forgiveness. Conversely, we should solidify our gratitude, like inscriptions on stone, enduring and unerasable. Embrace this duality of life, and you will find harmony in relationships and inner peace.

47. THE PERILOUS PATH OF INFLUENCE

"The best way to find yourself is to lose yourself in the service of others." – Mahatma Gandhi

In the Bollywood movie "Sanju," the protagonist Sanju's life unfolds, revealing the tumultuous journey marked by his struggle with addiction. A significant turning point in his life is his encounter with Zubin Mistry. Zubin, disguised as a friend, introduces Sanju to a destructive world of drugs. This encounter happens on a film set where Sanju, overwhelmed by nervousness and the pressure of performing well under his father Sunil Dutt's direction, seeks solace in smoking a cigarette offered by Zubin. Little does he know that this act marks the beginning of his downward spiral.

Zubin, under the guise of friendship, leads Sanju into the abyss of addiction, introducing him to a range of drugs like marijuana, hashish, LSD, heroin, cocaine, and various inhalants. Sanju, naively trusting Zubin, even refers to him as 'god'. However, Zubin's betrayal becomes evident as he himself consumes only glucose powder, while dragging Sanju deeper into drug dependency.

The severity of the situation dawns on Sanju during his time in a rehabilitation centre in America. Battling severe withdrawal symptoms and the urge to escape, Sanju faces his demons head-on. Upon his return to India, a reformed and self-determined Sanju encounters Zubin again. This time, however, Sanju stands firm, rejecting Zubin's attempts to drag him back into the world of drugs.

***

Sanju's story is a stark reminder of the perils of misleading influences and the strength it takes to overcome them. It highlights the importance of discernment in friendships and the power of self-will in battling addiction and reclaiming control of one's life. It serves as a cautionary tale about the dangers of succumbing to peer pressure and the transformative power of making positive life choices. His journey of overcoming addiction underscores the power of resilience and self-determination.

48. LINCOLN'S HUMBLE PRIDE: A LESSON IN DIGNITY

"I am not bound to win, but I am bound to be true. I am not bound to succeed, but I am bound to live up to what light I have." – Abraham Lincoln

Abraham Lincoln, as the newly elected President of the United States, stood before the Senate, ready to deliver his first presidential address. Among the attendees was an aristocrat who sought to undermine Lincoln's authority. As Lincoln prepared to speak, the aristocrat stood up and loudly remarked, "Mr. President, you should not forget that your father used to make shoes for my family." His words echoed through the chamber, intending to belittle Lincoln by reminding him of his humble origins.

The Senate erupted in laughter, thinking they had succeeded in making a mockery of Abraham Lincoln. However, Lincoln's response was not one of embarrassment or anger. Instead, he addressed the man with his characteristic humility and wit. "Sir, I am well aware that my father made shoes for your family, and for many others here," Lincoln began. "He was an unmatched cobbler who put his heart into his work. I wonder, do you have any complaints about his shoes? If so, I can make another pair, as I too am a skilled cobbler. But I know this: no one has ever complained about my father's shoes. I am proud of my father and my lineage!"

***

Lincoln's dignified response showcased his ability to confront ridicule with grace and pride. He not only defended his father's honour but also demonstrated the integrity and resilience that would come to define his presidency. His humble pride in his origins and his father's craftsmanship left the Senate speechless, revealing a profound lesson in dignity and respect. Remember, it is not our origins but our actions that define our true worth.

49. THE LAST RIDE

"Kindness is a language which the deaf can hear and the blind can see." – Mark Twain

In the deep silence of the night, a cab driver arrived to pick up his passenger, an elderly woman standing outside a building with a suitcase. He greeted her with a smile, assisted with her luggage, and courteously opened the car door for her. Once settled, she requested a drive-through downtown before reaching her final destination, the hospice. Understanding the gravity of her journey, the driver compassionately turned off the metre.

As they meandered through the city streets, the woman narrated the stories of her life. She pointed out the building where she grew up, the office where she spent her working years, and the spot where she met her husband. The cab driver listened, his attention a comforting presence in the quiet night.

Their journey continued for 2 hours, unfolding like a tapestry of memories against the backdrop of the city. As dawn broke, they arrived at the hospice, greeted by nurses. The driver carried her suitcase and watched as she was seated in a wheelchair.

When she inquired about the fare, he refused payment, stating, "Nothing at all." "You have to make a living," replied the woman. His response was heartfelt, "There are other passengers." Moved by the moment, he gave her a hug, an act of human connection that transcended the usual boundaries of a driver and passenger. Her gratitude was palpable as she expressed how much this final journey meant to her, a small act of kindness that brought a moment of joy to the end of her life's journey.

***

The story of the cab driver and the elderly woman is a touching reminder of the impact of kindness. In his simple, compassionate act, the driver brought a moment of joy and comfort to someone at the end of their life. This story encourages us to practise empathy and compassion in our daily interactions, understanding that sometimes, a small gesture can make a significant difference in someone's life.

50. THE LIGHT OF TRUTH

"The only true wisdom is in knowing you know nothing." – Socrates

In a bustling city, under the glow of a streetlight, a policeman noticed a dishevelled man searching on the ground. This man, whose eyes shimmered with the haze of intoxication, was looking for something lost. The officer, moved by a sense of duty and compassion, approached him.

"What are you looking for?" the policeman inquired gently.

"My keys," the man slurred, his gaze fixed on the ground.

Together, they scoured the area under the streetlight, shuffling through leaves and debris, but their search was fruitless. After a few minutes, the officer, puzzled, asked, "Are you certain you lost them here?"

The man paused, his throat momentarily clearing as he confessed, "No, I lost them in the park."

Perplexed, the officer asked, "Then why search here?"

"Because this is where the light is, it is dark out there." the man replied.

***

Often, we search for truth and wisdom in places illuminated by convenience and comfort, neglecting the darker, more challenging areas where they may truly reside. The light of the streetlamp, like the allure of easy answers, may guide us momentarily, but it's in the unlit paths of our journey where the keys to deeper understanding and enlightenment are found. Seek truth not where it's easiest to search, but where it's hardest to find. Embrace the journey into the unknown, for it is there that wisdom and truth await.

51. JOURNEY TO INNER PEACE

"The journey of a thousand miles begins with one step." – Lao Tzu

Sophia, a young woman, lived a life seemingly full of accomplishments, yet she felt an emptiness inside. Her days were spent chasing success, material possessions, and societal approval. However, beneath this facade, Sophia grappled with a growing sense of anxiety, a feeling of being lost in a world that valued external achievements over inner peace.

The turning point came when her anxiety reached its peak. Realising the need for change, Sophia embarked on a transformative journey. She turned inwards, seeking the wisdom of mindfulness, meditation, and self-discovery. This path was not easy; it required her to confront her deep-seated fears and negative thought patterns.

Sophia also sought guidance from a wise therapist, who helped her peel back the layers of societal conditioning. Through these sessions, she learned to appreciate the beauty of her inner world. Gradually, Sophia began to replace her negative thoughts with more positive perspectives, finding strength and confidence within herself. This journey led Sophia to a profound realisation: true fulfilment and power come from within. No longer driven by external validation, she found joy in her self-discovery.

***

Discover your inner strength like Sophia. Your journey to fulfilment is within, not in external validations. Embrace self-discovery, confront your fears, and transform anxiety into a source of power. Trust in your inner voice and find peace and joy in being true to yourself. Remember, the most profound journey is the one that takes you inside, to the core of who you are.

52. THE PRECIOUS VASE

"One of the hardest decisions you'll ever face in life is choosing whether to walk away or try harder." – Ziad K. Abdelnour

In a quaint home, a young boy named Robert found himself in a peculiar situation. He had curiously put his hand inside an antique vase, a precious heirloom from his grandmother, and now, to his dismay, he couldn't withdraw it. His worried mother, witnessing his struggle, called for her husband.

The father, calm and collected, tried various methods to free his son's hand. He applied soapy water, then vegetable oil, hoping to ease the hand out of the vase's narrow neck. Despite these efforts, Robert's hand remained stuck.

In a moment of frustration, the father exclaimed, "I'd give a dollar to get that hand out!" Suddenly, they heard a clinking sound, and Robert's hand slid out effortlessly. To their astonishment, a penny fell from the vase. Robert explained that he had been clutching the penny inside the vase, but upon hearing his father's offer, he let it go.

***

Often, we hold onto trivial things, unaware that they prevent us from experiencing greater opportunities and freedom. Just like Robert clinging to the penny, we sometimes hold onto beliefs, grudges, or fears, hindering our progress and well-

being. Let go of the 'penny' in your life to grasp something far more valuable. Release the trivial and embrace the significant. Embrace change, let go of the past, and open your hands and heart to the limitless possibilities that await.

53. THE VALUE OF SELF-WORTH

"The price of anything is the amount of life you exchange for it." – Henry David Thoreau

A father noticed that his son was constantly comparing himself with other children and having a low image of himself. To teach him a lesson about human worth, he handed his son a simple stone, instructing him to understand its value without saying a word, only showing 2 fingers when asked for its price.

First, the son went to the market. An old woman offered 2 dollars for the stone, which surprised the boy. He returned to his father, who then directed him to a museum. There, a man in a suit offered $200 for the same stone. Astonished, the son again went back to his father.

Finally, the father asked his son to visit a precious stone store. At the store, an old man, recognising the stone's true value, offered $200,000. Overwhelmed, the son rushed home to share the news with his father.

The father then revealed the essence of the lesson: "You see, son, the value of your life is all about where you place yourself. You can decide if you want to be a $2 stone, a $200 stone or a $200,000 stone. Some people will value you immensely, seeing your true worth, while others may see you as just another commodity. It is up to you to decide the value of your life."

***

Recognise your worth like the stone in the story. You are not defined by others' perceptions but by your own self-value. Do not settle for being undervalued or underestimated. Place yourself where you are appreciated and respected. Remember, your worth is intrinsic and priceless. Like the stone, you possess a unique value that only those with true insight can see. Believe in yourself and your worth, and the world will recognise it too.

54. FIND YOUR HAPPINESS

"Happiness is not something ready-made. It comes from your own actions." – Dalai Lama

In a thought-provoking classroom experiment, a teacher brought a collection of balloons to school. Each student received two balloons, inflated them, wrote their name on them, and released them into two empty classrooms. The balloons were then mixed up, creating a colourful chaos.

Taking the students to the first classroom, the teacher issued a challenge: *"Find your own balloon within five minutes."* This challenge created chaos; students frantically searched, colliding, and pushing each other, resulting in most balloons being destroyed. Unsurprisingly, no one found their balloon.

Seeing their frustration, the teacher took them to the second classroom and offered a new instruction. "Pick up any balloon and give it to the person whose name is written on it." This simple change in approach worked wonders. Within minutes, every student held their own balloon.

The teacher then shared a valuable lesson: "These balloons are like happiness. We will never find it if everyone is looking for their own. But if we care about other people's happiness, we find ours too." The story taught the students that happiness isn't a solitary pursuit. It's found in helping others, in the shared joy of giving and receiving.

***

Find happiness not by seeking your own but by bringing joy to others. When you uplift others, you uplift yourself. By shifting our focus from a self-centred search to a collective effort of caring and helping, we not only bring joy to others but also find our own happiness in the process. True contentment comes from selflessness and compassion. Remember, in the pursuit of happiness, the greatest fulfilment lies in making others happy.

55. THE POWER OF "I AM"

"Words have power. Words are power. Words could be your power." – Mohammed Qahtani

In a motivational session, a speaker shared a powerful concept with a young audience, focusing on the phrase "I am." He explained how these simple words shape our identity and destiny.

He began by asking, "Who are you?" The audience members thought of their names, families, and backgrounds. The speaker pointed out that beyond these external identifiers, there's a deeper aspect of self, unaffected by external circumstances, memory loss, or even physical changes. This core self is always present, acknowledging its existence.

The speaker emphasised that each person has the divine right to choose who they want to be. He urged the audience to decide from that moment who they are. "Say to yourself, 'I am a success, I am healthy, I am good, I am strong, I am happy, I am wealthy,'" he suggested. He stressed that the "I am" is at everyone's disposal, and they should hang every desired attribute on it.

However, he warned about the negative use of "I am," reminding them that many unconsciously label themselves with negativity, like "I am an idiot," "I am stupid," "I am worthless," or "I am poor." He encouraged them to consciously choose positive affirmations, as the "I am" doesn't discriminate and manifests whatever follows it, whether positive or negative.

***

Embrace the power of 'I am.' You can define and shape your life with your words and thoughts. Choose positive affirmations and believe in them. Remember, your self-perception shapes your reality. Don't limit yourself to negative thoughts. Instead, affirm your strengths, your hopes, and your dreams. Let 'I am' be the beginning of a powerful narrative of success, happiness, and fulfilment in your life. You are what you believe yourself to be.

56. FLIGHT TO SUCCESS

"The most difficult thing is the decision to act, the rest is merely tenacity." – Amelia Earhart

In a lush forest, a young bird named Timmy struggled with learning to fly. While his siblings soared effortlessly, Timmy could only hop on the ground, feeling embarrassed and discouraged. His inability to fly made him feel isolated, as he watched others enjoy the freedom of the skies.

One day, Timmy encountered Oliver, an old and wise owl known for his wisdom and kindness. Timmy confided his struggles to Oliver, who listened patiently before offering sage advice. He told Timmy that every bird starts on the ground and that learning to fly requires time, effort, and patience. Oliver suggested that Timmy start small by flapping his wings and jumping higher each day.

Motivated by Oliver's words, Timmy practised diligently. Each day, he flapped his wings and jumped, growing stronger and more confident. Finally, the day came when he felt ready to take off. With a burst of energy, he ran, flapped his wings, and lifted into the air. He was flying!

***

Timmy's success was not just in flying but in the journey that led him there. He learned to be patient, to persevere through challenges, and to embrace the process of growth. His journey taught him that success takes time and effort, and it's okay to make mistakes along the way. Timmy's transformation from a grounded bird to a confident flyer is a testament to the power of hard work, determination, and the courage to seek guidance.

57. THE RACE OF COMPASSION

"Success is not measured by what you accomplish, but by the opposition you have encountered, and the courage with which you have maintained the struggle against overwhelming odds." – Orison Swett Marden

In a small village, there lived a young, athletic boy, hungry for success and obsessed with winning. During a village running competition, he easily defeated his peers, basking in the glory of his victories. However, an old wise man, observing the races, remained unimpressed by the boy's triumphs.

For the next race, the wise man challenged the boy with unusual competitors: an elderly, frail lady and a blind man. Confused and indignant, the boy questioned the fairness of such a race. Yet, the wise man insisted, and the race began. Predictably, the boy finished alone, with the crowd remaining silent, offering no applause or praise.

Perplexed by the crowd's reaction, the boy sought answers from the wise man, who challenged him to run the race again, this time with a different objective: finish the race together with his challengers. The boy, understanding the lesson, took the old lady and the blind man by the hands and walked slowly with them to the finish line. This time, the crowd erupted in cheers and applause.

The wise man explained to the boy that life isn't just about winning or beating others. True success lies in helping others and running the race of life with compassion and empathy. It's about crossing the finish line together, celebrating collective victories rather than individual conquests.

***

In life, the greatest victories are those shared with others. Learn to run the race of life with compassion and empathy. Success isn't about crossing the finish line first, but about helping others get there too. Embrace the journey with a heart full of kindness and celebrate collective achievements. Remember, the most rewarding race is one where we lift each other and cross the finish line together.

58. GRATITUDE

"Gratitude turns what we have into enough, and more. It turns denial into acceptance, chaos into order, confusion into clarity." – Melody Beattie

Once, a hunter, deep in the jungle, lost his way while pursuing a deer. For 3 days, he wandered, hungry and despairing, unable to find an exit or sustenance. On the brink of hopelessness, a miraculous sight appeared: an apple tree, laden with fruit. Overwhelmed with gratitude, he gathered apples, their sweet taste a symbol of life's unexpected gifts.

The first apple was a divine relief, filling him with immense joy and thankfulness. But as he consumed the second, the third, and the fourth, his gratitude waned. By the fifth apple, his delight diminished noticeably, and by the tenth, he even started discarding those that seemed less flavourful, his sense of appreciation fading into discontent.

This transformation exemplifies the "Tenth Apple Effect" – a decline in gratitude as abundance becomes commonplace. The hunter, initially overjoyed, soon took the tree's bounty for granted, a pattern all too familiar in our lives. Each apple, as sweet as the first, lost its charm not due to its taste, but due to the hunter's shifting perspective.

***

In life's jungle, we often overlook everyday miracles, succumbing to the 'Tenth Apple Effect'. Let's cherish each 'apple' life offers with consistent gratitude. Remember, the sweetness of life's gifts doesn't diminish; our appreciation does. Embrace every moment with thankfulness, for in gratitude lies the true joy of living.

59. THE JOURNEY TO TRUE JOY

"Joy is what happens to us when we allow ourselves to recognise how good things really are." – Marianne Williamson

Ken Behring, an American entrepreneur and billionaire, narrated his life's transformation in a speech. He described his journey through 4 stages, each defined by his pursuit of happiness through material possessions and achievements.

In the first stage, Behring sought happiness in the "Right Stuff" – luxurious houses, cars, boats, and an aeroplane. Despite acquiring these, contentment eluded him. Moving to the second stage, he aimed for "Better Stuff" – upgrading his possessions to more lavish versions. Yet, happiness remained a distant dream.

The third stage was about "Different Stuff." Behring co-owned the Seattle Seahawks, believing that this unique achievement would finally bring joy. However, the void persisted. It was during this phase that a friend invited him to Europe to distribute wheelchairs to children with disabilities. This experience became a turning point.

Behring's first encounter was with an eleven-year-old boy who, after being placed in a wheelchair, clung to him and tearfully expressed a desire to thank him again in heaven. This moment of pure, unadulterated joy led Behring to the fourth stage, which he termed "Heavenly Stuff."

He founded the Wheelchair Foundation, providing over 750,000 wheelchairs worldwide. This act of giving, more than any material possession, filled him with genuine joy and fulfilment. In his own words, seeing the happiness in the recipients' eyes was his life's greatest achievement.

***

"True joy is found not in possessions, but in giving. Ken Behring's life teaches us that happiness is a journey from material fulfilment to altruistic contentment. Let's embrace the 'Heavenly Stuff' of life, finding joy in kindness, compassion, and making a difference in others' lives."

60. INTEGRITY OVER POWER

"Integrity is doing the right thing, even when no one is watching." – C.S. Lewis

The movie "A Man for All Seasons" exemplifies St. Thomas More's profound commitment to integrity and moral conviction. More, a gifted writer, lawyer, and judge, rose to prominence in 16th-century England, eventually becoming Chancellor under King Henry VIII. However, his life took a dramatic turn when the King sought to divorce Catherine of Aragon, marry Anne Boleyn, and declare himself head of the Church of England.

Thomas More, a man of deep faith and principle, believed the King's actions were against divine will. Faced with a moral dilemma, more chose his conscience over his prestigious position, resigning from his role as Lord Chancellor and embracing a life of poverty. His refusal to support the King's actions led to his arrest and imprisonment in the Tower of London in 1534.

The most striking moment came when Lord Norfolk presented more with a document, urging him to declare the King's remarriage lawful. Despite immense pressure and the allure of royal favour, more stood firm in his conviction. His iconic response, "I am the King's good servant, but God's first," echoed his unyielding dedication to his faith and principles. This unwavering stance ultimately led to his execution for treason on July 6, 1535.

***

St. Thomas More's life reminds us that true integrity is not swayed by power or position. His steadfast commitment to his principles, even unto death, serves as a beacon of moral courage. Let us draw inspiration from his example, prioritising our values and convictions over worldly gains, and remember that our deepest loyalty must always be to truth and righteousness.

61. SISTER MARIE'S ACT OF MERCY

"Forgiveness is the fragrance that the violet sheds on the heel that has crushed it." – Mark Twain

In 1832, Paris was gripped by a cholera epidemic. Amidst this crisis, Sister Marie, a Sister of Charity, devotedly served at a local hospital. One day, while on her way to the hospital, she encountered a workman who hurled insults at her, following her with foul language and almost resorting to physical violence, if not for the intervention of bystanders. Unperturbed, Sister Marie continued on her path, embodying the virtue of patience and forgiveness.

Days later, a new patient, critically ill with cholera, arrived at the already overcrowded hospital. The hospital officials, overwhelmed by the sheer number of patients, were turning him away when Sister Marie, passing by, recognised him. It was the same man who had insulted her. Displaying extraordinary compassion, she intervened, insisting, "Oh don't send him away! I will find a corner for him somewhere – I will look after him myself!"

She cared for him tirelessly, alongside her other patients, embodying selfless love and mercy. The man, unaware that Sister Marie was one of those he had previously insulted, slowly recovered under her diligent care. However, on the eighth day, when he inquired about her, he was informed that Sister Marie had contracted cholera herself and passed away the previous night.

***

"Sister Marie's life exemplifies the power of forgiveness and compassion in the face of adversity. Her act of caring for the one who wronged her teaches us to look beyond personal grievances and serve with love and mercy. Let her story inspire us to act with kindness, even when faced with hostility, embodying the true spirit of selfless service."

62. THE HUMANITY AMIDST WAR

"The smallest act of kindness is worth more than the grandest intention." – Oscar Wilde

In a poignant scene from the novel "All Quiet on the Western Front," the brutality of war collides with a moment of profound humanity. Amid a fierce battle between French and German soldiers, a young German soldier, after a ceasefire, finds himself in a shell hole. In a reflex of fear and survival, he fires at an unarmed French soldier. Approaching the dying man, he expects to feel triumph, but instead, he's confronted with the soldier's humanity – frightened eyes, parched lips, and a half-open mouth.

This sight stirs something unexpected in the German soldier – compassion. Overcoming the barriers of war and nationality, he offers his enemy a final act of kindness: a drink of water. As the French soldier succumbs to his wounds, the German soldier's initial sense of victory turns to sorrow. This was the first man he had killed. Curious about the man's identity, he searches his pockets, finding a wallet with family photographs – a woman and a little girl.

This discovery shatters the soldier's perception of the enemy. The French soldier was not just a foe; he was a father, a husband, a human being with loves and losses akin to his own. Overwhelmed by this realisation, the German soldier copies down the dead man's address, resolving to write a letter to his widow. In a pledge of ongoing compassion, he commits to send half his salary to the bereaved family every month.

***

In the face of war's dehumanising chaos, a young German soldier's act of compassion reminds us of our shared humanity. His realisation that the enemy is also a loved one to someone else teaches us empathy and kindness, even under the most trying circumstances. Let this story be a call to remember our common humanity, transcending barriers and extending compassion, especially when it's most challenging.

63. UNWAVERING FAITH IN TURBULENT TIMES

"Faith is not belief without proof, but trust without reservation." – D. Elton Trueblood

The story unfolds on a cross-country flight, where a pastor and his fellow passengers encounter a severe storm. The plane, battered by thunder and lightning, becomes akin to a cork tossed on a tumultuous ocean. Passengers are engulfed in fear, many praying or crying, as the aircraft experiences violent drops and rises.

Amidst this chaos, the pastor notices a striking contrast: a little girl, seated calmly, engrossed in her book. Her serenity amidst the surrounding turmoil is baffling. She alternates between reading and closing her eyes, her demeanour untouched by the fear gripping everyone else.

***

Curious, the pastor waits to speak with her after the plane lands. When asked why she wasn't worried during the storm, the girl reveals a profound truth: "My daddy is the pilot. And he's taking me home." Her unwavering faith in her father's abilities granted her peace that eluded the other passengers. Her trust was not in the stability of the flight or the absence of danger but in the hands guiding the plane.

***

In life's turbulent journeys, let the story of the little girl on the stormy flight remind us of the power of unwavering faith. Her serene trust in her father, the pilot, symbolises the peace we find when we place our trust in a God who governs this universe. Let us navigate life's storms with the same calm assurance, knowing that we are guided safely, even amidst chaos.

64. A LESSON IN HEEDING WARNINGS

"Heeding warning signs before tragedy strikes is the hallmark of wise decision-making." – Anonymous

In its day, the Titanic was the world's largest ocean liner, weighing 46,328 tonnes, and it was considered unsinkable. Yet, late during the night of April 14-15, 1912, the unthinkable happened to the unsinkable. Near midnight, the great Titanic struck an iceberg, ripping a three-hundred-foot hole through 5 of its 16 watertight compartments. It sank in 2 and a half hours killing 1,513 people.

Before the Titanic sank, warning after warning had been sent to tell the crew that they were speeding into an ice field, but the messages were ignored. In fact, when a nearby ship sent an urgent warning, the Titanic was talking to Cape Race about the time the chauffeurs were to meet arriving passengers at the dock in New York, and what dinner menus were to be ready. Preoccupied with the trivia, the Titanic responded to the warning, "Shut up. I am talking to Cape Race. You are jamming my signals!"

Why did so many die that night? Perhaps the crew disregarded the danger of the weather; there were not enough lifeboats on board; and the radio operator of nearby California was off duty; perhaps those responsible did not heed the warnings; they were preoccupied with other things!

***

Sometimes we believe that our 'ship' is unsinkable, our life is completely planned, and the unthinkable can never happen. We need to read the signs of the times; we need to pay attention to the warning signals. But if we are preoccupied with the trivial things of life, we will miss the most important things until it is too late. Stay vigilant and attentive.

65. THE LAST LEAF

"Hope is being able to see that there is light despite all of the darkness." – Desmond Tutu

In O. Henry's touching tale "The Last Leaf," the theme of hope in desperate times unfolds through the character of Johnsy, who is gravely ill with pneumonia. Lying in her bed, she becomes fixated on an ivy vine outside her window, firmly believing that her fate is tied to the leaves clinging to it. As the leaves fall one by one, her despair deepens, convinced she will die when the last leaf drops.

During a particularly harsh storm, Johnsy, resigned to her fate, awaits the inevitable fall of the final leaf. But in the morning, to her astonishment, it remains, defying the storm's fury. This unexpected sight sparks a change in her; hope flickers alive, and she begins to recover.

Behrman, an elderly artist living in the same building, aware of Johnsy's condition, braved the stormy night. With his brushes and paints, he crafted a realistic leaf on the wall, indistinguishable from the real ones. This act of artistic dedication became Behrman's masterpiece, a testament to his empathy and the transformative power of hope.

Tragically, Behrman caught pneumonia that night and passed away. But his final creation, a simple painted leaf, achieved something profound – it rekindled a young woman's will to live, showcasing the incredible strength and resilience of the human spirit when inspired by hope.

***

O. Henry's 'The Last Leaf' teaches us that hope can be a powerful force, even in the darkest of times. Behrman's selfless act of painting a leaf to inspire Johnsy reminds us that sometimes, the smallest gestures can have the most significant impact. Let this story be a reminder to always hold onto hope and to be that beacon of hope for others, even in the simplest of ways.

66. A TALE OF TWO SEAS

"Life's most persistent and urgent question is, 'What are you doing for others?'" – Martin Luther King Jr.

There are 2 unique bodies of water in the Middle East: the Dead Sea and the Sea of Galilee, both fed by the River Jordan, yet starkly different. The Dead Sea, renowned for its high salt content, supports no marine life. Its saltiness, about 10 times that of normal ocean water, renders it inhospitable to fish, vegetation, or any sea animals, thus earning its name.

In contrast, the Sea of Galilee, located just north of the Dead Sea, teems with vibrant marine life. It's home to over 20 different types of fishes, along with a rich variety of plants. What causes this stark difference, despite having the same source of water?

The answer lies in their respective ecosystems. The Sea of Galilee receives water from the River Jordan, which then flows out, allowing a constant exchange and renewal. This inflow and outflow of water sustains its healthy, dynamic environment, filled with life.

On the other hand, the Dead Sea lies far below sea level with no outlet. Water from the River Jordan flows in but has no exit route. Evaporation of over 7 million tonnes of water daily leaves behind a high concentration of minerals and salt, making it unsuitable for life.

***

This contrast between the 2 seas offers a profound metaphor for life. The Dead Sea, which only takes in water without giving, is lifeless. In contrast, the Sea of Galilee, which both receives and gives, is vibrant and alive. This story illustrates the importance of not just receiving but also giving in life, emphasising the vitality that comes from a balanced flow of giving and receiving.

67. THE POWER OF APPRECIATION

"Appreciation can make a day, even change a life. Your willingness to put it into words is all that is necessary."
– Margaret Cousins

Growing up in correction homes, Bob Danzig yearned for someone to love and appreciate him. His life took a pivotal turn at 9 when a new warden told him, "You are worthwhile!" These words, unheard of in his life before, echoed as an affirmation of his worth.

As a teenager, Bob graduated and took up a job as a copyboy at the Albany New York Times. Six months into his job, a crucial meeting with his boss, Margaret, was set to change his life again. Fearing dismissal, Bob was instead met with words that would fuel his aspirations – "You are full of promise." Margaret's belief in his potential empowered Bob to aim higher.

These affirmations became his mantra, guiding him through life's challenges and igniting a belief in his capabilities. His journey from a copyboy to the Publisher of the Albany New York Times, and eventually the CEO of Hearst Newspapers, one of the world's largest newspaper companies, was a testament to the transformative power of positive reinforcement. Bob Danzig's rise to success, fuelled by the appreciation and belief shown by others, exemplifies the impact a few encouraging words can have.

***

Bob Danzig's transformation from a neglected child to a successful CEO highlights the immense power of appreciation and belief. His story teaches us that words of encouragement can profoundly impact someone's life and self-worth. Let this story inspire us to recognise and appreciate the potential in others, understanding the lasting impact our words can have. Remember, a simple expression of belief can ignite a journey of success and self-discovery.

68. THE REWARD FOR HOSPITALITY

"Kindness is the language which the deaf can hear and the blind can see." – Mark Twain

On a stormy night many years ago, an elderly couple arrived at a small hotel seeking shelter. The clerk at the reception, aware that the hotel was fully booked due to 3 conferences in town, faced a dilemma. Despite the lack of rooms, he couldn't bear to send the couple out into the storm at such a late hour. Demonstrating remarkable kindness, he offered them his own room to sleep in.

The couple, initially hesitant, accepted the offer after the clerk insisted. The next morning, as the man tried to settle the bill, the young clerk refused payment. In a heartfelt moment, the elderly man told the clerk, "You're the kind of manager who should be the boss of the best hotel in the United States. Maybe someday I'll build one for you." The clerk smiled, amused by what he thought was a light-hearted joke.

Years passed, and then one day, the clerk received a letter from the elderly man, reminiscing about that rainy night and inviting him to New York, with a round-trip ticket enclosed. Upon arrival, the clerk was astounded to be taken to a grand new building at the corner of 5th Avenue and 34th Street. The elderly man revealed that this magnificent structure was the hotel he had built for the clerk to manage.

Incredulous, the clerk asked the man's identity, only to discover he was William Waldorf Astor. The hotel was the original Waldorf-Astoria, destined to become one of the most prestigious hotels in New York, and the young clerk, its first manager, was George C. Bolt.

***

The story of the Waldorf-Astoria's inception teaches us the enduring impact of kindness and belief in others. A simple act of compassion by a young clerk led to the birth of a legendary hotel, reminding us that our actions, however small, can have profound and unforeseen consequences. Let this tale inspire us to act with kindness and generosity, knowing that such virtues can pave the way for unexpected opportunities and remarkable destinies.

69. LIFE IS THE WAY YOU LOOK AT IT

"Gratitude turns what we have into enough." – Aesop

Walking down a rural road, 2 farmers engaged in a conversation that revealed a profound contrast in their outlooks on life. The first farmer, when asked how he was doing, lamented the harshness of his circumstances. He complained about the hard ground, the age of his cows, and the diminished sweetness of the milk. In his eyes, everything was terrible, life was unbearable, and there seemed to be no silver lining.

The second farmer, facing similar challenges, offered a remarkably different perspective. He acknowledged the hardness of the ground but expressed gratitude for having land to cultivate, recalling days when he had none. For him, hard ground was better than no ground. His cows, though old, still produced milk that found its way to the market. He appreciated what he had – his health, the ability to work, and the joy of doing what he loved. His response was imbued with a deep sense of gratitude and a recognition of the blessings in his life, despite the hardships.

***

The contrasting perspectives of the 2 farmers teach us the importance of gratitude, even in difficult times. While one dwells on the negatives, the other finds reasons to be thankful, illustrating how our mindset can greatly influence our experience of life. This story reminds us to practise gratitude, focusing on what we have rather than what we lack. Embracing gratitude can transform our outlook, making life's challenges more bearable and infusing our daily experiences with a sense of contentment and joy.

70. TO YOURSELF BE TRUE

"Every man is guilty of all the good he did not do."
– Voltaire

The King went to visit the prisoners in the state prison. He then asked each criminal what he was punished for. The King was surprised when each criminal pleaded innocence. There were many of them who said, 'I was framed;' 'They ganged up on me;' 'It was a case of mistaken identity.' Others instead blamed the police and the judges for their atrocities and biassed judgements, and the witnesses who gave false evidence.

One convict, however, acknowledged his wickedness openly. He said he deserved the punishment.

The King was touched by his sincerity. 'This man is too wicked to be with such innocent people. He must leave this place at once,' he said. He asked the judge to try him again and set him free.

***

The story of the sincere convict amidst deniers teaches us the value of honesty and accepting responsibility for our actions. It illustrates that owning up to our mistakes, even when others don't, can lead to unexpected opportunities and growth. Let this story encourage us to embrace truthfulness and accountability in our lives, understanding that genuine self-reflection and honesty can pave the way for forgiveness, redemption, and ultimately, a better future.

71. LOVE BEYOND MATERIAL POSSESSIONS

"The best things in life aren't things." – Art Buchwald

A young couple, after years of saving, finally realised their dream of buying a family car – a Maruti. The husband, particularly fond of the car, meticulously cared for it, washing and wiping it daily to keep it spotless. The car was his pride, and he made sure it remained without a scratch, a symbol of their hard work and savings.

One day, the wife took the car out for shopping. On her way back, she met with an accident, colliding against a bus. The impact was severe; the headlights and windscreen were smashed. Overwhelmed by the accident and the damage to the car, she was in tears, dreading her husband's reaction. The car he so dearly cared for was now in ruins.

Amidst this turmoil, as the checking Inspector requested the insurance papers, she found a small note hidden among them. The note, written by her husband, read: 'In case of an accident Honey remember it's you that I love and not the car.' This simple, heartfelt message changed everything. It was a poignant reminder that their love for each other surpassed any material possession, even something as cherished as their dream car.

***

The Maruti car story beautifully illustrates that in relationships, love and understanding transcend material possessions. The husband's note to his wife in times of an accident shows that it's the people in our lives who hold the true value, not the things we own. Let this story remind us to cherish our loved ones above all, understanding that material possessions are fleeting, but the bonds we share with those we care for are irreplaceable.

72. WINNING APPROVAL

"In the end, it's not the applause, but the journey that matters most." – Unknown

A young, aspiring violinist, having honed his skills under a world-renowned master, faced the pinnacle of his early career – his first major public recital in a large city. His journey to this moment was paved with dedication and an unyielding pursuit of musical excellence. As he stepped onto the stage, his heart raced, not just with nerves but with a deep desire to prove his worth.

With each piece he performed, the young violinist poured his soul into the music, his fingers dancing across the strings with skill and passion. The audience, musically astute and discerning, responded with overwhelming applause and shouts of "Bravo." Yet, amidst this sea of acclaim, the young man seemed almost aloof, as if the applause fell on deaf ears.

His eyes, throughout the performance, were fixed on one spot – the first row of the balcony. There, seated amidst the crowd, was his teacher, the master who had sculpted his talent. As the final notes of the last piece resonated through the hall, the applause was thunderous. But it was the gentle nod and smile of approval from his teacher that brought the young violinist true joy and relief. In that moment, he knew he had succeeded.

***

The young violinist's performance illustrates that often, our greatest achievements are validated not by public acclaim, but by the approval of those we respect and admire. His story reminds us of the importance of mentors in our lives and the unique fulfilment that comes from earning their respect. Let this story inspire us to seek validation not just from the crowd but from those who guide us, understanding that their acknowledgement is a true measure of our success.

73. A LESSON IN VALUE AND RESPONSIBILITY

"Price is what you pay. Value is what you get." – Warren Buffett

A teenage girl, captivated by a fancy Levi's jacket in a store window, saw it as the perfect attire for her college week event. Overwhelmed by the desire to own it, she rushed into the store, picked her size, and bought it without a second thought about the price. The moment of truth struck at the cashier when the price far exceeded her expectations. In a desperate move, she secretly emptied her father's wallet to cover the cost.

Proudly wearing her new jacket at the college week inauguration, she anticipated admiration and envy from her peers. Instead, she found herself walking alone; her friends distanced themselves, unimpressed by her display. That day, she returned home in tears, her joy turned to sorrow.

As she lay in bed, reflecting on the day's events, a critical question lingered in her mind, "Was the outfit worth that much?" The fancy jacket had come at a high cost, not just in terms of money, but also in the loss of respect from her friends and the guilt of having taken money without permission.

In the months that followed, this experience became a profound learning moment for the girl. She realised the importance of understanding the value of things and the responsibility of making purchases. "What does it cost?" became her new mantra, a question that extended beyond financial implications to encompass the ethical and personal costs of her decisions.

***

The tale of the girl and her Levi's jacket teaches a crucial lesson about understanding value and responsibility. Her experience reminds us that the allure of material possessions should be weighed against their true cost – financially, ethically, and personally. Let this story inspire us to consider the broader implications of our choices and to act with consideration and responsibility, understanding that the true cost of something is often more than its price tag.

74. A ROLE MODEL'S AWAKENING

"To the world, you may be one person, but to one person, you may be the world." – Dr. Seuss

While walking through the streets, Greg Louganis, an Olympic diving champion, encountered a young boy with a cigarette in his mouth. Louganis, concerned, asked the boy why he chose to smoke. The boy's response was unexpected and eye-opening: "Sir, because you do. You are my hero, and I want to be like you."

This encounter served as a wake-up call for Louganis. Until then, he hadn't fully grasped the impact of his actions on his admirers, especially young fans. The realisation that his habits, particularly smoking, were being emulated by a child who saw him as a hero, weighed heavily on him. The boy's words echoed in his mind, a clear indication of the kind of influence he had as a public figure and a champion.

Motivated by this encounter, Louganis decided to quit smoking. He recognised that being a role model extended beyond his achievements in diving; it also encompassed his lifestyle and choices. He understood that his actions, both in and out of the sporting arena, were being closely watched and often imitated by his fans.

Louganis' decision to stop smoking and adopt a healthier lifestyle wasn't just for his own benefit. It was a conscious effort to embody the qualities of a true role model, to be someone worthy of emulation in all aspects of life.

***

Greg Louganis' encounter with the young boy highlights the profound impact of role models in shaping behaviours and attitudes. It reminds us that our actions have far-reaching effects, especially on the young who look up to us. Let this story inspire us to be mindful of our actions and to strive to be positive role models, understanding the significant influence we hold in guiding the values and choices of the next generation.

75. RABBI NAFTALI'S AWAKENING

"Your work is to discover your work and then with all your heart to give yourself to it." – Buddha

In a quaint Russian village in the last century, the wealthy safeguarded their properties by hiring night watchmen. One evening, Rabbi Naftali, meandering near one such property, encountered a watchman. Curious, he inquired, "For whom are you working, young man?" The watchman named his employer but, with a hint of profundity, retorted, "And you, Rabbi, for whom are you working?" This simple question struck Rabbi Naftali with the force of revelation, prompting deep introspection.

After a moment of contemplative silence, Rabbi Naftali admitted, "At the moment, I am not working for anyone." This realisation led him to an unusual proposition. He asked the watchman if he would consider becoming his servant. Intrigued, the watchman eagerly agreed, inquiring about his duties. Rabbi Naftali's response was as profound as it was simple: "You will have to remind me every now and then for whom I am supposed to work."

Rabbi Naftali, a spiritual leader, was reminded of his deeper calling and responsibility beyond the worldly roles he played. The watchman's role transcended physical guarding; he became a guardian of the Rabbi's spiritual focus, a reminder of his true service and purpose.

***

The interaction between Rabbi Naftali and the watchman highlights the importance of self-reflection and remembering our true purpose. It reminds us to regularly question for whom and for what we are working, ensuring our efforts align with our deepest values and goals. Let this story inspire us to seek reminders that keep us grounded in our true purpose, understanding that amidst life's busyness, a moment of reflection can bring clarity and renewed dedication to our most meaningful pursuits.

76. THE WISDOM OF SIMPLICITY

"Life is really simple, but we insist on making it complicated." – Confucius

In the last century, an American tourist visited Rabbi Hofetz Chaim, a revered Polish sage. Expecting to find a home befitting a man of his stature, the tourist was startled to see that the Rabbi's abode was nothing, but a modest room lined with books, its only furnishings a table and a bench.

Curiosity piqued, the tourist inquired, "Rabbi, where is your furniture?" Hofetz Chaim, with a calm and reflective demeanour, returned the question, "Where is yours?" The American, somewhat bemused, responded, "Mine? But I'm only a visitor here. I'm only passing through." The Rabbi, with profound simplicity and depth, replied, "So am I."

This exchange, brief yet powerful, encapsulates a profound philosophy. Rabbi Hofetz Chaim's response was not mere rhetoric but a reflection of his life's philosophy. His spartan lifestyle was a conscious choice, rooted in the belief that physical possessions are transient, much like our time on Earth. His words conveyed a deeper understanding of life, viewing our earthly existence as a temporary journey, a transient phase before moving on to a higher, eternal realm.

***

Rabbi Hofetz Chaim's minimalist lifestyle and his poignant conversation with the tourist teach us the transient nature of our earthly existence and the futility of material attachments. His wisdom encourages us to reflect on our life's priorities, urging us to seek fulfilment in spiritual and intellectual growth rather than in material wealth. Let this story be a reminder to cherish what truly matters and to live a life rich in purpose and simplicity.

77. THE MIRROR OF PERCEPTION

"We do not see things as they are, we see them as we are." – Anaïs Nin

Once upon a time, in a serene village nestled in the heart of nature, 2 newcomers arrived on separate occasions, each seeking a new beginning. The first, carrying the weight of past grievances, approached a local tourist guide with a question that reflected his inner turmoil. "Do you think I will like it in this village? Are the people nice?" he inquired.

The guide, perceiving the man's outlook, replied, "How were the people in the town where you came from?" The newcomer described them as "nasty, greedy, angry, and deceitful." The guide, with a knowing look, said, "Those are exactly the type of people we have in this village."

The next day, another newcomer visited the guide with the same question. This individual, however, carried a different aura, one of positivity and hope. When asked about his previous town's inhabitants, he spoke fondly of them, describing them as "sweet, harmonious, caring, respectful, and spiritually inclined."

To this, the master responded, "Well, those are exactly the type of people we have in this village."

This tale illustrates a profound truth: our perception of the world reflects our inner state. The first man, burdened with negativity, saw only the worst in people, whereas the second, filled with optimism, saw the best. It's a reminder that the world is a mirror, reflecting our thoughts, attitudes, and beliefs. The story teaches us to cultivate a positive outlook, for what we see in the world, the world will see in us.

***

Your perception shapes your reality. Choose to see hope, goodness, and love, and the world will reflect these qualities back to you. Like the newcomers in the story, your outlook determines the world you experience. Embrace positivity, kindness, and compassion, and you'll find these virtues mirrored in your surroundings. Remember, the world is your mirror; what you project, reflects.

78. A LIFE'S MISDIRECTION

"In the end, we will remember not the words of our enemies, but the silence of our friends." – Martin Luther King Jr.

As an old man lay on his deathbed, a sense of unease clouded his final moments. A friend, sitting beside him, sensed his turmoil. Breaking the heavy silence, the old man recounted a childhood memory that had haunted him for years. He spoke of a field near a crossroad where he used to play as a boy. There stood an old signpost, a guide for travellers at the intersection of 2 roads.

In a mischievous act of youth, the boy had once twisted the signpost, altering its directions. The arrows, which were meant to guide, now pointed travellers down the wrong paths. As he neared the end of his life, the old man was troubled by the thought of how many people he might have misdirected, not just with that single act but through other misguided actions throughout his life.

This story is a poignant reflection on the consequences of our actions, both big and small. The old man's regret over a childhood prank symbolises a deeper introspection into the impact of our choices on others. It underscores the often-unforeseen ripple effects our actions can have, shaping the lives of others in ways we may never fully comprehend.

***

The old man's story is a sobering reminder that our actions, even those that seem insignificant, can have far-reaching consequences. It urges us to live with consideration and awareness, understanding that what we do can impact others in profound ways. Let this story inspire us to act responsibly and thoughtfully, be mindful of the paths we pave for ourselves and others, and to seek to correct our misdirection's before it's too late.

79. THE POWER OF FORGIVENESS

"To love another person is to see the face of God."
– Victor Hugo, "Les Misérables"

Victor Hugo's "Les Misérables" presents a profound narrative centred around Jean Valjean, a man sentenced to 19 years in prison for stealing bread for his starving family. His life takes a pivotal turn when he escapes and seeks shelter in a kind bishop's house, only to betray the hospitality by stealing silver candlesticks. Captured and brought back to the bishop, Jean Valjean braces for the worst, expecting to be condemned.

However, the bishop's response is unexpectedly merciful. Instead of accusing Jean, he greets him as a friend and claims that the candlesticks are a gift. This act of unexpected kindness leaves Jean in a state of emotional turmoil, marking the first time in 19 years that he has shed tears. The bishop's compassion doesn't end there; he urges Jean to use the candlesticks to start a new, honest life.

This moment of forgiveness becomes the catalyst for Jean's transformation. Heeding the bishop's words, Jean embarks on a journey of repentance, gradually reshaping his life. His transformation is so profound that he eventually becomes the mayor of his town, embodying dignity and respect.

***

Jean Valjean's transformation in 'Les Misérables' demonstrates the life-altering impact of forgiveness and compassion. His story is a reminder that everyone has the potential for redemption and that acts of kindness can lead to profound personal growth. Let this story inspire us to practise empathy and forgiveness, understanding that our capacity to forgive can not only change others' lives but also enrich our own with deeper understanding and humanity.

80. A TALE OF FREEDOM AND LOYALTY

"Freedom is not the absence of commitments, but the ability to choose – and commit myself to – what is best for me." – Paulo Coelho

In the era before the abolition of slavery, a poignant tale unfolded involving Abraham Lincoln and a young slave girl. Lincoln, known for his compassionate and just nature, embarked on a noble act that would forever change the girl's life. He purchased her from a slave dealer, not for servitude, but to grant her the gift of freedom.

As Lincoln handed the girl her papers of freedom, she was enveloped in a mix of surprise and disbelief. Years of bondage had conditioned her to view herself merely as an object of trade, making the concept of freedom alien to her. "You are free," Lincoln told her gently. Her response was one of pure amazement, "Free? Can I go wherever I want to go now and do whatever I want to do?" Lincoln affirmed, assuring her of her newfound autonomy.

In that moment of realisation, the girl's reaction was both unexpected and profound. Instead of choosing to explore the world as a free individual, she made a decision that reflected her deep gratitude and respect. "Then," she declared, "I shall stay with you and serve you until I die." Her decision to stay with Lincoln was not born out of obligation or coercion but out of a genuine sense of loyalty and appreciation for the man who had granted her the most precious gift – freedom.

***

Lincoln's act of liberating a slave girl and her choice to remain with him teach us about the true essence of freedom and gratitude. The story illustrates that sometimes, the greatest loyalty is born from acts of kindness and compassion. Let this tale remind us that the bonds we form through our actions can be stronger than any obligation and that true freedom includes the freedom to choose whom we honour and serve out of love and gratitude.

81. A STORY OF LOVE AMIDST LOSS

"Sometimes, the most powerful thing you can say is nothing at all." – Mandy Hale

In a small, happy home, a long-awaited joy came with the birth of a boy to a loving couple. The boy, a beacon of their love, was cherished deeply. However, a routine morning turned tragic when the father, rushing to work, noticed an open medicine bottle. He asked his wife to safely store it, but amidst her morning chores, she forgot.

The boy, drawn to the bottle's colour, consumed its contents – a potent medicine intended for adults in small doses. The poison's effect was immediate and devastating. The mother, in a state of panic, rushed her son to the hospital, but it was too late. The child passed away, leaving her in a vortex of guilt and fear, especially about facing her husband.

When the husband arrived at the hospital, confronted with the unbearable sight of his lifeless son, his reaction was not of anger or blame. Instead, he looked at his wife, who was drowning in guilt, and offered her 5 words of profound compassion and support: "I am with you, Darling." He embraced her, providing solace in the midst of an unspeakable tragedy.

This story is a heartbreaking yet powerful testament to the strength of love and support in the darkest of times. The husband's response to the tragedy exemplifies unwavering compassion and understanding, recognising that their shared loss was a time for solidarity, not blame. In a moment where words fall short, his actions spoke volumes, offering a beacon of hope and unity in the face of despair.

***

The tragic story of the couple and their loss is a poignant reminder of the power of empathy and support in times of sorrow. It shows how, in the face of unimaginable grief, the presence and understanding of a loved one can provide immense comfort. Let this story inspire us to offer unwavering support to those in need, understanding that sometimes, the greatest gift we can give is our presence and unconditional love in the darkest moments.

82. A WINDOW OF OPPORTUNITY

"Education is the most powerful weapon which you can use to change the world." – Nelson Mandela

In 1860, in Vignola, Italy, a young boy's curiosity and desire for learning caught the attention of a school teacher. Standing outside, peering through the window in the cold, the nine-year-old boy, Ludovico Antonio Muratori, was observed by the teacher, who initially tried to keep his pupils focused on their lessons. Intrigued by the boy's persistence, the teacher inquired about his unusual presence at the window.

Tearfully, Ludovico explained that he hadn't done anything wrong; he was merely there to listen and learn, as his father couldn't afford the 6 liras for his studies. Challenged by the teacher to prove his attentiveness to previous lessons, Ludovico demonstrated an impressive recall of the material. Astonished, the teacher invited him to join the class, promising to resolve the issue of the tuition fees.

The opportunity to study in the classroom marked a turning point in Ludovico's life. His remarkable progress by the end of the year was just the beginning of an extraordinary journey. With the help of charitable individuals, Ludovico continued his education, eventually becoming a great scholar, a professor of history, and a noted Italian writer.

***

Ludovico Antonio Muratori's story is a powerful reminder of the life-changing impact of education and the importance of seizing opportunities. His journey from an eager boy outside a classroom to a renowned scholar underscores the potential in every child, regardless of their circumstances. Let this story inspire us to support and encourage the pursuit of knowledge, understanding that a small act of kindness can unlock a world of potential and change the course of a person's life.

83. THE UNSEEN STRENGTH OF THE FATHER

"Love is the strongest force the world possesses, and yet it is the humblest imaginable." – Mahatma Gandhi

Anthony Castle recounts a harrowing incident involving V. Backman and his family. After enjoying a pleasant picnic at the beach, a day of joy turned into a nightmare in a split second. As Backman prepared to leave, he was jolted by the scream of his four-year-old son. His heart sank as he realised the unthinkable: in backing up the car, he had accidentally run over his own child.

In a moment of sheer panic and desperation, Backman, a man weighing only 130 pounds, confronted a seemingly impossible task. The car, a massive 3000-pound vehicle, had one of its wheels pinning his son underneath. Driven by a primal surge of adrenaline and love, Backman did the unthinkable. He grabbed the car's bumper and, with a strength he never knew he possessed, lifted the vehicle high enough to free his son.

This incredible feat, born out of a father's love, highlights the extraordinary power that love can unleash. In the face of such an extreme situation, Backman tapped into an immense reservoir of strength, fuelled by his deep love and instinct to protect his child. The incident stands as a testament to the idea that love is not just an emotion but a powerful force capable of driving us beyond our perceived limitations.

***

The story of V. Backman's heroic act underscores the extraordinary strength that love can evoke in times of crisis. It reminds us that in moments of extreme stress, especially when the welfare of a loved one is at stake, we can access remarkable inner strength. Let this story inspire us to recognise the immense power of love, understanding that it can transform us and empower us to perform extraordinary feats beyond our ordinary capabilities.

84. A STORY OF A CHILD'S SIMPLE WISH

"The greatest gifts you can give your children are the roots of responsibility and the wings of independence."
– Denis Waitley

In a tale recounted by Lovasik, a busy doctor experienced a heart-warming encounter with his young son that offered a profound lesson in the simplicity of a child's desires. Engrossed in his work in his study, the doctor was interrupted by the quiet presence of his son, who stood silently by his side, seeking his attention.

Assuming that the boy wanted something material, the doctor instinctively reached into his pocket, pulling out a coin to offer to his son. However, to his surprise, the boy gently refused the money, stating, "I don't want any money, Daddy." Perplexed but still preoccupied, the doctor then opened a drawer and presented a bar of chocolate to the boy, hoping this would satisfy his need. Yet again, the child declined the treat, maintaining his position by his father's side.

Growing slightly impatient and unable to fathom what his son could possibly want, the doctor turned to him with a look of exasperation and asked, "Well, what do you want then?" The boy's response was simple yet profound: "Nothing," he replied, a little confused. "I only want to be with you!"

***

This touching interaction sheds light on the often-overlooked emotional needs of children. The doctor's son sought nothing more than his father's company and attention, a desire far more valuable to him than any monetary or material offering. It's a poignant reminder of the importance of being present and available for our loved ones, recognising that sometimes, all they really want is our time and presence.

85. THE PRICE OF TIME

"Time is the most valuable thing a man can spend."
– Theophrastus

Aaron, with timid eyes, inquired of his father, "Daddy, how much do you make an hour?" The father, weary from a long day's work and surprised by the question, dismissed his son's curiosity. But the boy persisted until the father, somewhat reluctantly, revealed his hourly wage: 20 dollars.

Aaron's next request, for a loan of 10 dollars, agitated his father further, leading to a harsh rebuke. Aaron retreated to his room, silenced and disheartened. Later, reflecting on his harsh response, the father felt remorseful and approached his son, offering the requested 10 dollars. To his surprise, Aaron pulled out another 10 dollars from under his pillow, explaining that he now had enough to "buy" one hour of his father's time.

***

This heartrending exchange between the father and son serves as a powerful reminder of the value children place on time spent with their parents. The boy's desire to "purchase" his father's time was a heartfelt plea for attention, highlighting the often-unspoken emotional needs of children. The father's initial reaction, driven by fatigue and misunderstanding, turned into a moment of realisation about the importance of being present for his child.

86. A FATHER'S PRECIOUS PROMISE

"The greatest gift you can give someone is your time because when you give your time, you are giving a portion of your life that you will never get back." – Unknown

A young, successful attorney fondly recalled the greatest gift he ever received, a gift that came in a small, light box one Christmas. Inside the box was a note from his father that read, "Son, this year will give you 365 hours. An hour every day after dinner is yours. We'll talk about what you want to talk about, we'll go where you want to go and play what you want to play. It will be your hour!"

True to his word, the father devoted an hour every day to his son, engaging in whatever activity or conversation the son chose. This promise, simple yet profound, became a cherished ritual between father and son. It wasn't the discussions or the games that mattered most; it was the undivided attention and the bond they forged in those daily hours.

As years passed, the father renewed this promise annually, demonstrating his unwavering commitment to his son's growth and happiness. This continuous investment of time and attention played a pivotal role in shaping the young man's character and outlook on life.

***

The attorney credited this gift of time as the foundation of his success. It wasn't just the accumulation of hours, but the quality of connection, understanding, and love that these hours represented. The father's gesture was a powerful testament to the enduring impact of parental involvement and the priceless value of time spent together. Let this story inspire us to make time for our loved ones, understanding that these moments of connection and shared experiences are foundational to their growth, happiness, and cherished memories that last a lifetime.

87. A MOTHER'S BELIEF AND THE BIRTH OF A STAR

"Behind all your stories is always your mother's story, because hers is where yours begins." – Mitch Albom

Many years ago, in Naples, a ten-year-old boy harboured a dream to become a singer. His aspirations faced a crushing blow when his first music teacher dismissed his talents, saying, "You can't sing. You haven't any voice at all. It sounds like the wind in the shutters." This harsh critique could have ended his pursuit, but the boy's mother, a simple peasant woman, believed fiercely in her son's potential.

With unwavering faith and love, she encouraged him, telling him not to lose heart. She saw something in him that others did not – a budding talent that just needed nurturing. In her eyes, he could already sing, and she saw improvement where others saw none. Determined to support her son's dream, she went to great lengths, even going barefoot to save money for his music lessons.

Her sacrifices and steadfast belief in her son's abilities transformed his life. Her encouragement became his anchor, pushing him to persevere and refine his skills. That young boy was Enrico Caruso, who would grow up to become one of the most celebrated opera singers of his time.

***

Enrico Caruso's story is a poignant reminder of the profound impact a parent's belief can have on a child's life. His mother's unwavering faith and support in the face of adversity propelled him from humble beginnings to global fame. Let this story inspire us to believe in and encourage the potential in others, understanding that our faith and support can be the catalyst that turns dreams into reality and nurtures talent into greatness.

88. FROM TRAGEDY TO SERVICE

"Desire is the starting point of all achievement, not a hope, not a wish, but a keen pulsating desire which transcends everything." – Napoleon Hill

Anita Paul's life as a doctor in a government hospital, known for her selfless service to the poor, was deeply influenced by a childhood tragedy. Born into poverty, Anita experienced a life-altering event when her mother fell seriously ill. With no medical facilities nearby, her family's desperate attempt to seek help led to a harrowing journey to a neighbouring village, 8 km away by bullock cart. Tragically, her mother died en route, a loss that profoundly impacted young Anita.

This experience left an indelible mark on Anita, fuelling a resolve that would shape her future. She understood the pain of losing a mother at a young age and the helplessness of not having access to medical care. Determined to prevent such tragedies in her community, Anita made a vow to herself: that she would become a doctor.

Years of hard work and dedication followed, leading her to fulfil her vow. Anita became a beacon of hope and healing in her town, dedicating her life to serving those in need. Her days off were spent in the slums, providing care to those who otherwise had no access to medical help. Her journey from a child affected by tragedy to a committed doctor serving the underprivileged is a story of resilience, compassion, and dedication to a cause greater than oneself.

***

Anita Paul's journey from personal tragedy to a life of service as a doctor exemplifies the power of turning sorrow into a force for positive change. Her story teaches us that our most challenging experiences can inspire us to make a difference in the world. Let her dedication remind us to channel our adversities into driving forces for our goals, understanding that we can transform our pain into meaningful action that betters the lives of others. Oprah Winfrey said, "Turn your wounds into wisdom."

89. DREAM THE IMPOSSIBLE

"Some men see things as they are and ask why. Others dream things that never were and ask why not." – George Bernard Shaw

In a classroom, an English teacher assigned her students the task of writing a fable. Among the submissions was Little Jimmy's story, a tale that defied the norms of nature but carried a profound message.

The story began with a turtle sunning itself on a riverbed. Suddenly, it noticed a crocodile nearby, its head emerging ominously from the water. Startled, the turtle swiftly slid off the log and paddled towards the shore. But the crocodile followed, its mouth wide open in anticipation.

As the turtle reached the bank, it found itself in an even more precarious situation. It ran as fast as it could, but the crocodile was close behind, gaining on the turtle with every moment. In a final, desperate attempt to escape, the turtle did something extraordinary – it climbed a tree. The crocodile, unable to follow, was left baffled below.

When the teacher read this fable, she commented, "Jimmy, this is an exciting tale, but it isn't true to nature. Crocodiles can't climb trees, but neither can turtles."

Jimmy's reply was simple yet profound: "But this one could. Heck! He had to."

Jimmy's story, while bending the laws of nature, conveyed an important lesson. It illustrated the power of necessity in driving one to adapt and overcome seemingly impossible obstacles. The turtle's unlikely action of climbing a tree symbolised the innate ability of beings to rise to challenges when faced with dire circumstances, embodying the spirit of survival and adaptability.

***

Jimmy's fable teaches us that necessity can inspire extraordinary actions. Just as the turtle in his story adapted to an impossible situation, we too can find innovative solutions in the face of adversity. This story is a reminder that sometimes, the impossible becomes possible when driven by the need to survive. Embrace adaptability and resilience, for they are the keys to overcoming the most daunting of challenges.

90. VALUE EDUCATION

"Education without values, as useful as it is, seems rather to make man a more clever devil." – *C.S. Lewis*

Social worker Padmini Muthuswamy narrated the heart-wrenching story of a crippled boy she discovered in a slum. Driven by a deep sense of compassion, she became invested in his well-being, aspiring to see him walk and live a life like other boys his age. Her efforts led her to consult renowned orthopaedic surgeons in Vellore, who agreed to assist. Following a series of operations and a painstaking recovery, the boy miraculously began to walk, then run, and eventually play like his peers.

Years passed, and the boy grew into a man. Padmini, reflecting on this journey, posed a question to her audience: "Guess where he is and what he is doing now." The audience speculated various noble professions – a doctor, a social worker, a priest, or an industrialist. But the reality was starkly different. Padmini revealed, "No, you are all wrong. He is in the central jail, serving a life-term for murder!"

This revelation was shocking and sobering. Padmini lamented, "We spent all our time teaching him how to walk but failed to show him which path to take." While they had focused on his physical rehabilitation, they neglected to guide him morally and spiritually. The boy, once a symbol of triumph over adversity, had tragically lost his way.

***

Padmini's story is a poignant reminder of the critical need for holistic development in nurturing young lives. It's not enough to heal the body; one must also guide the soul, teaching values and ethics to steer them towards a righteous path. We must endeavour to teach not just how to walk, but also which path to follow. Let's remember, true care involves nurturing the body, mind, and soul, guiding young lives towards a path of righteousness and integrity.

91. ACTION NOT WORDS

"The best way to find yourself is in the service of others."
– Mahatma Gandhi

Leslie Weatherhead recounts the touching tale of a young girl in a London hospital, drawing her final breaths. Orphaned at an early age, she dedicated her life to caring for her younger siblings, sacrificing her own health and well-being. Her hands, rough and red, bore the scars of her hard work and selfless love.

As death neared, a visitor approached her with a sombre question, "I suppose you know you're dying. What are you going to do when you stand before God?" The question hung heavily in the air, a stark reminder of the inevitable journey she was about to embark upon.

The girl remained silent for a moment, absorbing the gravity of the question. Her gaze then drifted to her hands, resting on the hospital bed's white coverlet. These hands, though marred by toil and sacrifice, were a testament to her life's work – a life spent in service to those she loved dearly.

With a soft smile, she replied, "I think I'll show Him my hands." In those few words, she conveyed a lifetime of love, sacrifice, and devotion. Her hands, marked by hardship, were her testimony; they told her story more eloquently than words ever could.

***

This young girl's story is a powerful illustration of the beauty and dignity in selfless service. Her hands, a symbol of her unwavering dedication, remind us that the true measure of our lives is often found in the sacrifices we make for others and the love we share. Her response to show her work-worn hands to God symbolises a life lived in service and love. Let us be inspired by her example to dedicate ourselves to acts of kindness and compassion, understanding that our greatest legacy lies in the positive impact we have on the lives of others.

92. DOING YOUR BEST

"Success is to be measured not so much by the position that one has reached in life as by the obstacles which he has overcome." – Booker T. Washington

Booker T. Washington's journey to education was a testament to his unyielding determination and resilience. As an African-American in a time of profound racial discrimination, Washington faced immense challenges in pursuing higher education. Undeterred, he set his sights on a university that accepted coloured students. The journey was not easy; he walked 4 hundred miles, fuelled by a burning desire for knowledge and a better future.

Upon arrival, his hopes were dashed when he learned that the university was full. No seat was available for him in the classrooms. However, instead of turning back, Washington accepted an offer to work at the university, sweeping floors and making beds. This job was far from what he had hoped for, but he embraced it with exceptional diligence and dedication.

Washington's work ethic did not go unnoticed. He swept the floors with such care and made the beds with such precision that he soon gained the respect and admiration of the university staff. His commitment and excellence in these humble tasks eventually opened the doors for him to become a student at the very university that initially turned him away.

Later in life, Booker T. Washington went on to found Tuskegee University in 1881. He led the institution until his death, rising to become one of the greatest men of his era. His story is a powerful illustration of perseverance, hard work, and the belief that no task is too menial if it leads to a greater goal. Washington's journey from a janitor to a respected educator and leader is an enduring inspiration.

***

Booker T. Washington's story exemplifies the power of determination and the dignity of labour. His unwavering commitment to his goals, even in the face of adversity, reminds us that perseverance and a positive attitude can transform obstacles into opportunities. Let's be inspired by his journey, understanding that every step, no matter how small, is a progression towards achieving our dreams. His life teaches us to embrace every opportunity as a stepping stone to greater heights.

93. SELF-SACRIFICE

"Compassion and tolerance are not a sign of weakness, but a sign of strength." – Dalai Lama

During a fierce battle in the Netherlands, Sir Philip Sidney, a distinguished British Commander, was gravely wounded. As he lay on the battlefield, rapidly losing blood, an intense thirst overcame him. Realising his dire need, the soldiers scrambled to bring him a glass of water, a scarce and precious resource in the heat of battle.

As Sidney lifted the glass to his parched lips, his eyes met those of a fellow soldier, also severely wounded. The soldier's gaze was fixed on the water, his eyes wide with a mix of desire and the unmistakable pain of impending death. Despite his own critical condition, Sidney was struck by the suffering of this soldier, a comrade in arms who shared the same brutal fate on the battlefield.

In a moment of profound compassion, Sidney made a decision that would immortalise his character in the annals of history. With a selfless gesture, he instructed his soldiers to give the water to the other man, uttering the words, "His need is greater than mine."

***

Sir Philip Sidney's selfless act amidst the chaos and horror of war, stood as a beacon of humanity. Sidney, a commander responsible for leading men into battle, demonstrated that the virtues of compassion and empathy transcend the savagery of warfare. His decision to prioritise the needs of another over his own, even in the face of death, remains a powerful testament to the enduring strength of the human spirit. Let's be inspired by his example, understanding that even in the most dire circumstances, acts of kindness and empathy can make a profound difference. His legacy urges us to always extend a helping hand, even in our own times of need.

94. THE GIFT OF LOVE

"To love one's neighbours, to love one's enemies, to love everything – to love God in all His manifestations."
– Leo Tolstoy

In ancient Ireland, a childless King decided to choose his successor from among his people. The only condition was that the candidate must demonstrate a deep love for God and neighbour. In a remote village, a kind-hearted youth, known for his generosity and helpfulness, was encouraged by his fellow villagers to enter the contest for kingship. They collected funds to support his journey to the royal palace, providing him with food and a good overcoat for the trip.

As the young man approached the castle, he encountered a beggar shivering in the cold, dressed in torn clothes and begging for food in the royal park. Moved by compassion, the youth gave his new overcoat and the food he had saved for his return journey to the beggar.

Upon reaching the palace and waiting for a long time, the youth was finally admitted for an interview with the King. As he raised his eyes after bowing before the King, he was astonished to see the King wearing the overcoat he had given to the beggar. The King, revealing himself as the beggar from the park, greeted the young man as the new King of the country.

The King's disguise was a test to find a successor with a true heart of compassion and selflessness. The young man's act of giving his overcoat and food to a beggar, despite his own needs, exemplified the virtues the King sought. His selfless love for his neighbour, even in a time of personal need, earned him the greatest reward – the throne.

***

The story of the Irish King and the compassionate youth teaches us the value of selflessness and empathy. True greatness lies not in power or wealth, but in the willingness to help others, even when it requires personal sacrifice. This tale encourages us to always act with kindness and compassion, as these virtues can lead to unexpected and profound rewards. Let us remember, the greatest measure of our character is how we treat those in need.

95. THE FLIGHT OF COURAGE

"Courage is not the absence of fear, but rather the judgement that something else is more important than fear." – Ambrose Redmoon

High atop a mountain lived a family of eagles, overlooking a village with a winding stream and distant farmland. One day, the mother eagle knew it was time for her young to learn to fly. "You must learn to fly," she declared. The young eagles, filled with uneasiness, questioned how. "Go to the edge of the cliff," she instructed, "and throw yourselves into the wind."

The young eagles approached the cliff's edge cautiously, peering down into the vast expanse below, and quickly retreated to the safety of their nest. Their fear was palpable, the unknown daunting. The next day, the mother eagle again insisted it was time for them to fly. Met with protests of the height and the fear of falling, she encouraged them, "Come to the edge, don't be frightened."

As they hesitantly approached the edge, the mother eagle knew what she had to do. With a gentle nudge, she pushed them from the nest. Startled, the young eagles instinctively spread their wings. To their amazement, the wind caught beneath their wings, lifting them into the sky. They soared, riding the currents of the air, their fear replaced by exhilaration.

This first flight was more than a lesson in flying; it was a lesson in courage and trust. The mother eagle's push was a necessary act of love, teaching her young ones that sometimes, to discover their potential, they must be nudged out of their comfort zone. It was a leap of faith for the young eagles, a trust in their wings and the wind, and a trust in the love and wisdom of their mother.

***

The story of the young eagles learning to fly teaches us the importance of courage and trust in facing life's challenges. Sometimes, we need a gentle push to leave our comfort zone and discover our true potential. Just like the eagles, we may feel fear when facing the unknown, but it's in these moments that we learn to spread our wings and soar. Embrace life's challenges with courage, and trust in your ability to rise above.

96. IT JUST BECAME A HABIT

"Tradition is not to preserve the ashes but to pass on the flame." – Gustav Mahler

A newlywed husband watched curiously as his bride prepared to cook a ham. Before placing it in the oven, she meticulously trimmed off both ends of the ham. Puzzled, the husband inquired, "Why did you do that? I've never seen anyone cut off the ends of a ham before cooking it."

The wife, equally perplexed, admitted, "I don't really know. That's how my mother always did it." Her curiosity piqued; she called her mother to ask about this unique method. The mother's response was similarly uncertain, "I don't know, dear. That's just how your grandmother always did it."

Determined to unravel this culinary mystery, the bride then called her grandmother. The grandmother chuckled as she explained, "Well, sweetheart, the first oven we owned wasn't big enough to fit a whole ham, so I had to cut the ends off to make it fit. After that, it just became a habit!"

This simple family tradition, passed down through generations without question, reveals the power and persistence of inherited practices. It illustrates how rituals and habits, often established out of necessity or circumstance, can become entrenched in family culture, even long after their original purpose has become obsolete.

***

The trimmed ham story highlights the importance of understanding the origins and reasons behind our actions and traditions. It reminds us that sometimes, we follow practices without knowing why, simply because they have been handed down to us. This tale encourages us to reflect on our habits and question their relevance in our lives today. Let's carry forward traditions with meaning and purpose and be open to change when it leads to better understanding and improvement.

97. DEAL WITH HABITS EARLY ON

"Our character is basically a composite of our habits. Because they are consistent, often unconscious patterns, they constantly, daily, express our character." – Stephen Covey

An elderly teacher and his pupil were walking through a forest when the teacher paused to illustrate a powerful life lesson. He pointed to 4 plants near them: the first barely emerging from the ground, the second more firmly rooted, the third a small shrub, and the fourth a full-sized tree. He then instructed the pupil to pull up the first plant, which the boy did with ease, using only his fingers.

Next, the teacher asked him to pull up the second plant. The youth complied but found the task more difficult. Then came the third plant, which required all the boy's strength to uproot. Finally, the teacher told the pupil to try his hand with the fourth plant, the full-sized tree. The boy grasped the trunk but couldn't even shake its leaves.

The teacher used this moment to impart a profound truth: "This, my son, is what happens with our bad habits. When they are young, we can remove them readily; but when they are old, it's hard to uproot them, though we pray and struggle ever so sincerely."

The ease with which the boy removed the first plant represented the simplicity of changing a new habit. As the plants grew in size and strength, so too did the difficulty in changing them, just like deep-rooted habits in our lives.

***

The story of the 4 plants teaches us the importance of addressing bad habits early. Like the plants, habits grow stronger and more entrenched over time, becoming increasingly difficult to change. This tale reminds us to be vigilant and proactive in our personal growth, cultivating good habits and addressing negative ones before they become unmanageable. Let's nurture positive behaviours from the start, understanding that early intervention is key to a life of good habits and character.

98. SHACKLETON'S CALL TO ADVENTURE

"Difficulties are just things to overcome, after all."
– Sir Ernest Shackleton

Years ago, The London Times published a small yet compelling advertisement: 'Men wanted for a hazardous journey. Small wages, bitter cold, long months of complete darkness, constant danger, safe return doubtful. Honour and recognition in case of success.' This honest and daunting call to adventure was issued by Sir Ernest Shackleton, a renowned polar explorer.

Remarkably, the advertisement drew over 5,000 applicants, a testament to the human spirit's longing for exploration and challenge. From this vast pool of hopefuls, Shackleton carefully selected 27 men to join him on an expedition to explore the South Pole.

This journey was fraught with peril. The crew faced unimaginable hardships: bitter cold, treacherous ice, and the ever-present threat of disaster. Despite the risks, Shackleton and his team pressed on, driven by a shared sense of purpose and the lure of the unknown.

Their journey was one of incredible endurance and bravery. Shackleton's leadership and the crew's unwavering commitment saw them through the darkest hours. Against all odds, the entire crew completed their journey and returned home to honour and recognition. Their safe return was not just a triumph over the harsh elements of the Antarctic but also a victory of human determination and resilience. This journey, perilous as it was, captivated the imagination of the world and etched the names of Shackleton and his crew into the annals of history.

***

Sir Ernest Shackleton's South Pole expedition exemplifies the power of courage and perseverance in the face of adversity. His story inspires us to embrace challenges, however daunting they may seem. The spirit of exploration and the pursuit of the unknown can lead to remarkable achievements. Let's remember that the most extraordinary journeys often begin with a single step of bravery, and it is our resilience and determination that carry us through to success and recognition.

99. WHAT ARE WE MADE OF?

"But the Lord said to Samuel: 'Do not look on his appearance or on the height of his stature, because I have rejected him; for the Lord sees not as man sees, man looks on the outward appearance, but the Lord on the heart.'" – Old Testament, 1 Samuel 16:7

In a bustling market, a balloon seller sought to captivate a crowd of children. With a flair for showmanship, he released helium-filled balloons into the air: a white one, then a red, followed by a yellow. Each balloon ascended gracefully into the sky, drawing oohs and aahs from the fascinated kids who rushed to buy these colourful wonders.

Among the crowd, a little African-American boy watched intently. After a moment of thought, he approached the balloon seller with a curious look in his eyes. "If you filled a black balloon, would it go up too?" he asked innocently.

The balloon seller, understanding the deeper implication of the boy's question, knelt down to his level. With a reassuring smile, he replied, "Sure, it would. It's not the colour of the balloon but what's inside that makes it rise. It was what was inside them – the helium that enabled them to rise."

***

The balloon seller's story is a beautiful illustration of the principle that it's what's inside us that counts, not our external appearance. This tale teaches us to look beyond superficial differences and recognise the inherent potential and worth in everyone. Let's remember that like the balloons, irrespective of colour, it's our inner qualities and values that enable us to rise and achieve great heights. True upliftment comes from within, not from our external characteristics.

100. CHANGE IS TOUGH

"God grant me the serenity to accept the things I cannot change, the courage to change the things I can, and the wisdom to know the difference." – Reinhold Niebuhr

In an effort to illustrate the dangers of alcohol, a speaker presented a dramatic demonstration to a group of alcoholics. He prepared 2 identical containers filled with clear liquids: one with pure water, the other with undiluted alcohol. The audience watched intently as the speaker began his experiment.

First, he placed a small worm in the container with water. The worm swam around, reaching the side of the glass, and then crawled to the top, unharmed and lively. The audience observed the worm's vitality, noting its unaffected state in the water.

Next, the speaker transferred the same worm into the container filled with alcohol. The reaction was immediate and shocking. The worm disintegrated right before their eyes, dissolving in the harsh liquid. The speaker, satisfied with the dramatic effect, turned to the audience and confidently asked, "There, what's the moral?"

A voice called out: "If you drink alcohol, you'll never get worms!"

The speaker meant to convey alcohol's toxicity. But the attendee interpreted events through his existing pro-drinking bias, reflexively resisting the intended message. We all filter input through our beliefs and perspectives –

even to our detriment. Preconceptions blind us to growth opportunities.

***

Clinging to rigid perspectives that reinforce what we wish to believe limits our ability to learn, even when lessons stare us plainly in the face. If we cannot open our minds, we cannot move forward. Progress demands the courage to challenge old assumptions, assess honestly, and admit falsehoods that once shaped us. True wisdom comes not from finding truths that suit us, but facing truths that change us.

101. KEEP GROWING

> *"Mount Everest, you beat me the first time, but I'll beat you the next time because you've grown all you are going to grow… but I'm still growing!" – Edmund Hillary*

In 1952, Edmund Hillary faced a formidable challenge: the ascent of Mount Everest, the world's highest peak. Despite his valiant efforts, he failed to reach the summit. Undeterred by this setback, Hillary returned home, where he made a significant declaration that would define his resolve. Drawing a picture of Everest, he proclaimed loudly, "Mount Everest, you beat me the first time, but I'll beat you the next time because you've grown all you are going to grow… but I'm still growing!"

This statement wasn't just an expression of determination; it was a testament to Hillary's belief in personal growth and the power of perseverance. His words captured the essence of his unyielding spirit and the conviction that obstacles, no matter how insurmountable they seem, can be overcome.

On May 29, 1953, Hillary's unwavering dedication bore fruit. He became the first person to successfully climb Mount Everest, standing atop the 29,028-foot peak, a symbol of human endurance and triumph. This achievement was not just a personal victory but an inspiration to all who dare to dream big.

A few weeks later, in a London stage appearance, he received a thunderous applause. Grasping the microphone, he shared his profound insight: "Hold on to your dreams, for they become realities because you are still growing." This message was a powerful reminder that personal growth and steadfast commitment to one's dreams are the keys to turning the seemingly impossible into reality.

***

Edmund Hillary's journey to conquer Mount Everest teaches us the power of perseverance and personal growth. His triumphant ascent after initial failure illustrates that with dedication and a belief in continuous improvement, we can overcome great challenges. His story encourages us to hold fast to our dreams and recognise that our potential for growth is limitless. Let us remember, in the face of adversity, that we are still growing and capable of achieving extraordinary feats.

102. HEARING THE VOICE OF GOD

"The most important thing a man can know is that, as he approaches his own door, someone on the other side is listening for the sound of his footsteps." – Clark Gable

In George Bernard Shaw's play "Saint Joan," a profound conversation unfolds between Joan of Arc and the Dauphin of France. Joan, known for her divine visions and the voices she claimed to hear from God, faces scepticism from the Dauphin. Frustrated, he exclaims, "Oh your voices, your voices! Why don't the voices come to me? I am King, not you."

Joan's response is insightful and enlightening. She tells the Dauphin, "They do come to you. But you do not hear them. You have to sit in the field in the evening listening for them. If you sincerely prayed from your heart and listened to the sound of the bells in the air after they stopped ringing, you would hear the voices as well as I do."

The Dauphin, preoccupied with his kingly duties and earthly concerns, is unable to attune himself to the subtler, spiritual messages that Joan receives.

***

The conversation between Joan of Arc and the Dauphin in 'Saint Joan' teaches the importance of stillness and openness to receive guidance. It reminds us that wisdom and guidance are available to all, but we must be willing to listen and attune ourselves to them. Let us seek quiet moments of reflection to hear our 'voices,' understanding that true guidance often comes in whispers, not shouts, and is heard best in the silence of a sincere heart.

103. SERVICE OF MANKIND

"I don't know what your destiny will be, but one thing I know: the only ones among you who will be really happy are those who have sought and found how to serve." – Albert Schweitzer

In Europe, there lived a young and handsome doctor renowned for curing millions of patients. His reputation for healing and compassion made him a figure of admiration, attracting attention far and wide. Among his many admirers was a beautiful girl who expressed her desire to marry him. However, the doctor's response was cautionary, "If you marry me, you will be sorry," he said, hinting at a hidden sorrow in his life.

Despite receiving hundreds of letters from women around the world, the doctor remained distant from romantic entanglements. His focus was solely on his medical mission. Then, one day, he penned a touching article in a newspaper, announcing his departure from the world. This farewell message left the public in shock and sorrow, as they grappled with the loss of a man who had contributed immensely to humanity.

The mystery of his departure was soon revealed in a local daily, which announced the doctor's death. Unbeknownst to all, the doctor had been battling cancer for years. In the face of his own suffering, he had selflessly dedicated his life to the service of others, putting their needs above his own.

His tireless efforts to heal and help, even as he endured his own pain, made him a true hero in the eyes of the world.

***

The selfless doctor's story is a poignant reminder of the profound impact of sacrifice and service. His dedication to healing others, even while enduring his own suffering, exemplifies true altruism. This tale inspires us to look beyond our struggles and dedicate ourselves to helping others. It teaches us that the greatest fulfilment often comes from selfless service, reminding us that in serving others, we often find the deepest sense of purpose and meaning in our own lives.

104. SHARING GOD'S LOVE

"The best portion of a good person's life is the little nameless, unremembered acts of kindness and love."
– William Wordsworth

In the heart of New York, a twelve-year-old boy, the only son of a wealthy millionaire, made a startling discovery. While sifting through an old file of newspaper clippings, he stumbled upon a headline that caught his eye: 'Millionaire adopts a foundling.' The article detailed how an unknown baby, found abandoned in a church porch, had been taken into the home of Mr. H, the boy's father. The date on the clipping was exactly 12 years ago.

Curiosity piqued, the boy ran to his father, waving the newspaper cutting. "Look Dad – tell me what became of this baby they found?" he asked, his eyes wide with intrigue. His father, enveloping him in a warm embrace, revealed a truth that would forever change the boy's understanding of his life. "That baby is you," he said gently. "Twelve years ago, when I heard you were lying in the orphanage unclaimed, I took the opportunity to share my life and wealth with someone else."

The revelation left the boy speechless. He was the foundling in the story, the child his father had chosen to love and raise as his own. Overwhelmed with emotion, he asked, "Are you glad you did it, Dad?" His father's response was immediate and heartfelt: "Yes indeed, I am very glad, my son." The boy, now aware of his extraordinary journey, embraced his father tightly, whispering, "I am so lucky, Daddy!"

***

This touching story is a profound testament to the power of love and destiny. It illustrates that family is not always defined by blood but can be forged through the selfless act of kindness and the willingness to open one's heart to another. This tale reminds us to cherish the relationships we have, understanding that love and kindness can create the most enduring and meaningful bonds. In love, we find our truest fortune. It is well said, "Family is not defined by our genes; it is built and maintained through love."

105. THE POWER OF MOTIVATION

"Believe in yourself and all that you are. Know that there is something inside you that is greater than any obstacle." – Christian D. Larson

In a verdant forest, 2 friends, a mynah and an elephant, shared a unique bond. The elephant, beholding the freedom of birds, longed to experience flight. He confided in the mynah, "All my life, I have dreamed of flying – to soar over the village, glide above the river, and explore the jungle from the skies. Do you think I can fly?"

The mynah, understanding the power of belief, crafted a plan. He plucked a feather from his tail and handed it to the elephant. "Take this feather, hold it firmly in your mouth, then flap your ears as hard as you can. You will fly," he assured.

With unwavering faith in his friend's words, the elephant placed the feather in his mouth and flapped his ears vigorously. Miraculously, he began to fly. He soared over the village, marvelled at the river from above, and brushed past the treetops. This extraordinary experience brought him joy and a sense of accomplishment he had never known.

Upon returning to Earth, the elephant expressed his gratitude to the mynah, crediting the feather for his newfound ability. The mynah revealed the truth: "That feather? It was just an old one of mine. You didn't need it. I gave you something to believe in. It was you who did it, not the feather." The elephant's flight was not the result of the feather, but of his own strength and determination, awakened by faith in himself.

***

The story of the flying elephant teaches us about the power of belief and self-confidence. Like the elephant who thought the feather enabled him to fly, we often attribute our successes to external factors. However, it is our own strength, determination, and belief in ourselves that truly propel us forward. Let's remember that our abilities and potential are not defined by external tokens but by our own inner conviction and the faith we have in ourselves.

106. OVERCOMING ADVERSITY

"It is impossible to live without failing at something, unless you live so cautiously that you might as well not have lived at all – in which case, you fail by default."
– J.K. Rowling

J.K. Rowling's journey from facing deep depression to becoming the world's richest author is a story of resilience, imagination, and triumph over adversity. The most traumatising moment in her life was the death of her mother when she was 25, a loss that deeply affected her and occurred 6 months after she began writing "Harry Potter."

Rowling's life took a challenging turn when she moved to Portugal, married, and soon found herself in a failing marriage. She divorced after 13 months and moved to Edinburgh with her daughter, Jessica. Rowling faced severe financial struggles, relying on state benefits and often writing in cafes while her daughter slept next to her in a pram. She described herself as jobless, a lone parent, and as poor as it was possible to be in Britain without being homeless.

During this period, Rowling fell into a deep depression, even contemplating suicide. However, her love for her daughter and the story of Harry Potter kept her going. She manually typed each version of her book to send to publishers, facing numerous rejections. Finally, Bloomsbury Publishing gave "Harry Potter" a chance, largely thanks to the CEO's eight-year-old daughter, who loved the book.

The "Harry Potter" series went on to sell over 450 million copies, win numerous awards, and be made into movies, transforming Rowling's life completely. By 2011, Forbes estimated her worth to be around $1 billion. Rowling's journey is a remarkable example of how perseverance, belief in one's story, and overcoming personal and professional obstacles can lead to extraordinary success.

***

J.K. Rowling's journey from a struggling single mother to a best-selling author is a powerful reminder of the strength of the human spirit. Her story teaches us that even in the depths of despair, determination and belief in one's dreams can lead to incredible success. Let Rowling's journey inspire us to persevere through challenges, holding onto our dreams and passions, and understanding that failure and rejection are merely stepping stones to success.

107. FOOTPRINTS OF GOD

"When I think of God, my heart is so full of joy that the notes leap and dance as they leave my pen, and since God has given me a cheerful heart, I serve Him with a cheerful spirit." – Franz Joseph Hayden

A French scientist, known for his scepticism about the existence of God, embarked on a journey through the deserts of North Africa. Accompanying him was a young Bedouin boy, who had grown-up amidst the vast expanses of sand and sky. As they travelled, the scientist, in his typical non-believing stance, remarked to the boy, "No one knows for certain whether there is a God."

As they trekked across the smooth stretch of sand, the boy noticed a track of footprints of animals and knew exactly which animal passed that way. Then, seeing a set of human footprints, he said to the scientist, "When I see these footprints, I know a man had passed this way. Only a man could have made them." His observation was simple yet profound. Then, gesturing towards the sky, where the sun was setting amidst a canvas of clouds and stars, the boy continued, "When I see the sun, the clouds, the stars, and all the wonderful beauty of this world, I know for certain that the Creator has passed this way. They are the footprints of God."

The scientist was taken aback by the boy's wisdom. Through his innocent yet insightful observation, the boy had articulated a powerful argument for the existence of a Creator. In the footprints on the sand and the majestic beauty of the natural world, the boy saw undeniable evidence of a higher power, a divine hand in the creation of the universe.

***

The Bedouin boy's insight in 'The Footprints of God' story teaches us to see the extraordinary in the ordinary. His interpretation of nature as evidence of a divine Creator reminds us that belief can often be nurtured by appreciating the beauty and intricacy of the world around us. This tale encourages us to look beyond the surface, to find deeper meanings and connections in our surroundings, and to be open to the possibility of a greater presence in our lives.

108. WHAT IS MOTIVATING YOU?

"When a goal matters enough to a person, that person will find a way to accomplish what at first seemed impossible." – Nido Qubein

A young boy, a reserve player on his school's soccer team, practised diligently while his father, who was blind, sat watching him from afar. When the time for the finals arrived, the boy hadn't been seen in practice or in the previous matches. Unexpectedly, he appeared for the final game, pleading with the coach to let him play. Despite his reservations, the coach, moved by the boy's earnestness, agreed.

The game commenced, and the boy played with unprecedented skill and fervour. He was unstoppable, shooting goal after goal, leading his team to a stunning victory. His performance was so extraordinary that it left the coach astounded. He approached the boy, asking what had changed, how he had played so exceptionally well.

The boy's response was simple yet profound: "Coach, my father is watching me today." The coach turned around and looked at the place where the boy's father used to sit. There was no one there. He said, 'Son, your father used to sit there when you came for practice, but I don't see anyone there today.'

The boy revealed a heart-wrenching truth: his father had passed away 4 days ago. "Coach, there is something

I never told you. My father was blind. Just 4 days ago, he died. Today is the first day he is watching me from above."

***

The story of the young soccer player and his father teaches us about the unseen yet powerful influence of love and belief. It shows how the unwavering support and faith of a loved one can inspire us to surpass our limitations and achieve greatness. This tale is a touching reminder that the ones we love continue to guide and motivate us, even after they are gone. In their memory, we find the strength to reach new heights.

109. THE UNIQUENESS OF EACH ONE

"It is the inside you that is important. Dress up and look good so you attract people who can find out how nice, interesting and valuable you are." – Patricia Fripp

A King, strolling through his garden one morning, was dismayed to find many of his plants withering and dying. Curious about this decline, he inquired of an oak tree near the gate why it was dying. The oak confessed its dissatisfaction with life, lamenting that it was not tall and beautiful like the pine. Similarly, the pine yearned to bear delicious fruits like the pear tree, while the pear tree envied the rose's fragrance.

This pattern of discontent was widespread throughout the garden, with each plant bemoaning its lack of another's qualities. However, amidst the widespread dissatisfaction, the King came upon a small, cheerful pansy. Intrigued, he asked the pansy why it was the only happy plant in the garden.

The pansy replied, "Your Majesty, I know I'm small and of no significance, but I realised that you wanted a pansy when you planted me. If you had wanted an oak or a pear tree, you would have planted one in my place. Therefore, I am determined to be the best pansy I can be."

The pansy's response was a revelation to the King. It underscored the value of contentment and recognising one's unique purpose. Unlike the other plants, the pansy embraced its role and flourished, understanding that the King had planted it for its unique beauty and qualities.

***

The King's Garden story teaches us the importance of contentment and recognising our unique value. Like the pansy, we should embrace our individual qualities and purpose, rather than comparing ourselves to others. This tale reminds us that happiness lies in accepting and being the best version of ourselves, not in longing for attributes we lack. Let's cultivate a spirit of gratitude for our unique traits and contributions, understanding that each of us has a special role to play in the tapestry of life.

110. LIFE IS FULL OF MIRAGES

"If most of us remain ignorant of ourselves, it is because self- knowledge is painful and we prefer the pleasures of illusion." – Aldous Huxley

Many years ago, when Egyptian troops first conquered Nubia, a regiment found themselves marching through the harsh Nubian Desert. With only limited water supplies, the soldiers suffered from extreme thirst. One blistering afternoon, they believed they saw a beautiful lake with an oasis several miles off their path. Convinced of its existence, they pleaded with their Arabian guide to lead them there.

However, the guide, familiar with the desert's deceptive nature, insisted that it was a mirage and urged them to stay on course. He knew the urgency of conserving their energy and water for the journey ahead. But the thirsty soldiers, driven by desperation and illusion, refused to heed his warnings. In the heated argument that ensued, the soldiers, blinded by their thirst and frustration, killed the guide – the very person whose knowledge was crucial for their survival.

Ignoring the guide's advice, the commander and his men headed towards the mirage. As they approached, the illusion of the lake dissipated, revealing the harsh reality of endless burning sand. One soldier, realising the dire consequences of their actions, penned in his diary: "Raging thirst and horrid despair! The pathless desert and the murdered guide...lost! Lost!" Tragically, none of the soldiers survived; their bodies were later found by a group of Arab guides, a testament to the folly of ignoring wise counsel for fleeting illusions.

***

The tragedy of the Nubian Desert soldiers teaches the vital importance of heeding wise counsel and resisting the allure of illusions. It serves as a cautionary tale about the dangers of allowing desperation and false hopes to override sound judgement. Let us remember to trust in the wisdom of those who guide us, understanding that sometimes what we desperately seek may be nothing more than a mirage, leading us away from our true path to safety and success.

111. ACHIEVING MASTERY

"The happiness of a man in this life does not consist in the absence but in the mastery of his passion." – Alfred, Lord Tennyson

According to legend, King Arthur, during the early days of his reign, often rode in search of adventures. His trusted adviser, Merlin, warned him of a forthcoming challenge: he would encounter a dwarf who would provoke a fight. Merlin advised that upon defeating the dwarf, Arthur should kill him to prevent future threats.

True to Merlin's prophecy, Arthur met the dwarf in the forest. After a skirmish, Arthur, the superior swordsman, disarmed the dwarf. When the dwarf pleaded for mercy, Arthur, in his benevolence, spared his life and let him go. Merlin, upon hearing this, expressed his disapproval, cautioning that the spared dwarf would eventually become a grave danger.

The following day, the dwarf reappeared, slightly taller and more formidable. Again, they fought, and again Arthur spared him. This pattern continued for 10 consecutive days. With each encounter, the dwarf grew in size and strength, until on the eleventh day, he had transformed into a giant. This giant savagely attacked Arthur, killing his horse and engaging him in a fierce battle. The conflict escalated, culminating in a deadly fight where Arthur, despite being gravely wounded, managed to defeat the giant, cleaving his skull.

***

King Arthur's encounter with the dwarf-turned-giant teaches the importance of addressing issues when they are small. Like Arthur's repeated mercy, our hesitancy to act decisively can allow minor problems to grow into major threats. This story reminds us that sometimes, mercy and forbearance, though noble, may not always be the wisest course of action. It encourages us to be vigilant and proactive in dealing with challenges before they escalate beyond our control.

112. OVER DEPENDENCE

"Everybody wants to be somebody; nobody wants to grow" – Johann Wolfgang Von Goethe

Once upon a time, along the beautiful West Coast of Monterey, a flock of pelicans thrived in a Californian paradise. These majestic birds had an easy life, thanks to the local fishermen. After cleaning their catch, the fishermen would generously toss the leftover entrails to the pelicans. This act of kindness turned into a routine, and the pelicans grew accustomed to this effortless feast.

Day by day, the pelicans became plumper and lazier, their wings seldom stretching to glide over the ocean's surface. They lived in a state of contentment, relying solely on the fishermen's daily offerings. However, as time passed, the fishermen discovered a commercial use for the fish entrails. No longer were they discarded; instead, they were collected and sold for profit.

The pelicans, unaware of this change, continued to wait for their free meals. Days turned into weeks, and the once bountiful entrails never came. The pelicans, enveloped in their past contentment, had forgotten the essential skill of fishing for themselves. They waited, growing thinner and weaker, their eyes glossing over with hunger. The instinct to dive into the ocean's depths, to hunt and survive, had faded.

Tragically, many of the pelicans succumbed to starvation. They perished not because the ocean lacked fish, but because they had forgotten how to fish. The art of self-reliance, once inherent in their nature, had been lost in the comfort of dependency.

Embrace self-reliance and remember your innate strengths. The story of the Monterey pelicans serves as a poignant reminder: Comfort can lead to complacency, and reliance on others can erode our self-sufficiency. An ancient proverb says, "Give a man a fish, and you feed him for a day. Teach a man to fish, and you feed him for a lifetime." In life, it's crucial to maintain our skills and independence, lest we forget how to fend for ourselves in times of change. Stay vigilant and adaptable, cherishing the ability to thrive independently.

113. THE PURPOSE OF LIFE

"Do not dwell in the past, do not dream of the future, concentrate the mind on the present moment."
– Buddha

In ancient Persia, a King, renowned for his quest for wisdom, summoned the 3 wisest men in his kingdom. He posed a profound question: "What is the greatest evil of life?" This question stirred the minds of the wise men, each deeply contemplating the essence of life and its pitfalls.

The first wise man, after much thought, spoke with a sombre tone, "Life's greatest evil is to be engulfed in debts, without the means to repay them." He argued that the burden of debt cripples one's freedom and ability to enjoy the fruits of life, casting a long shadow of worry and helplessness.

The second wise man, reflecting on human frailty, countered, "Of all evils, the most grievous is to be struck with an illness for which there is no cure." He emphasised the agony of enduring a sickness that robs one of vitality, leaving a person at the mercy of fate, without hope for recovery.

Finally, the third wise man shared his insight, "The greatest evil of life is to stand at its end, only to realise that it was wasted." He posited that living without purpose, failing to embrace life's opportunities, and reaching the end with a heart full of regrets, was the ultimate tragedy.

The King, absorbing their words, realised the depth of their wisdom. Each perspective offered a different lens to view life's challenges, emphasising the importance of financial responsibility, health, and living a life filled with purpose and fulfilment.

***

Reflect on the wisdom of the Persian court: Life's greatest evils – the burden of debt, incurable illness, and a life wasted. These teachings remind us to manage our resources wisely, cherish our health, and most importantly, live purposefully. Avoid the trap of existing without truly living. Embrace every moment, pursue meaningful goals, and leave no room for regret. A life well-lived is a life rich in experiences, love, and wisdom.

114. THE COIN OF DESTINY

"Destiny is not a matter of chance, it is a matter of choice; it is not a thing to be waited for, it is a thing to be achieved." – William Jennings Bryan

In a pivotal moment of Japanese history, General Nabunaga faced a daunting challenge. His army, greatly depleted, was on the brink of a critical battle. Despite the overwhelming odds, Nabunaga's confidence in victory was unshaken. However, his soldiers harboured doubts about their impending fate.

As they marched towards the battlefield, they paused at a Shinto Shrine, seeking divine intervention. Resuming their journey, Nabunaga decided to boost his soldiers' morale in an unconventional way. He announced, "I shall now toss a coin. If it is heads, we shall win; if tails, we shall lose. Destiny shall guide us." The coin spun in the air, eventually landing on heads. This surprising outcome ignited a newfound spirit within the troops. Fuelled by their bolstered morale, they fought fiercely, ultimately emerging victorious against their adversaries.

The day after their triumph, one of the captains, reflecting on the battle, remarked to Nabunaga, "No one can change destiny." Nabunaga, with a knowing smile, revealed the coin used for the toss. It was a unique coin, bearing heads on both sides! This revelation highlighted not just the role of destiny, but also the power of belief and confidence in shaping outcomes.

Nabunaga's clever tactic underscored a profound lesson: sometimes, the belief in victory can be as crucial as the strategy itself. By instilling confidence in his men, he turned the tide of the battle, demonstrating that the strength of spirit can triumph over the direst of circumstances.

***

General Nabunaga's story teaches us about the power of belief and confidence. A coin with 2 heads, a symbol of assured victory, transformed his soldiers' doubt into determination. This tale reminds us that often, our fate is not just a matter of chance, but also of our mindset. Theodore Roosevelt said, "Believe you can and you're halfway there." Believe in your capabilities, embrace confidence, and let it guide you to triumph over challenges. The greatest victories are often won first in the mind.

115. JUMPING INTO CONCLUSIONS

"You never really understand a person until you consider things from his point of view until you climb into his skin and walk around in it." – Harper Lee

In a bustling city, a curious incident unfolded on a crowded street. A man, dressed in simple clothes, hurried along the pavement, clutching a large bag under his arm. Close behind, a plump middle-aged woman ran frantically, seemingly in pursuit. A passerby, witnessing this scene, assumed a robbery and decided to intervene.

Driving a truck, the passerby skillfully manoeuvred to cut off the man's path, almost colliding with him. The sudden obstruction startled the man, who stopped abruptly. The woman, closing in rapidly, seemed just as surprised by the turn of events. In this moment of pause, both the man and woman appeared bewildered, their expressions reflecting a mix of fear and confusion.

However, the scene took an unexpected twist. Instead of confronting each other or seeking help, both individuals, still looking astonished, cautiously walked around the truck and boarded a waiting city bus. The passerby, left in a state of puzzlement, watched as the bus drove away, carrying the 2 mysterious figures.

This peculiar incident left more questions than answers. Was the man actually a thief, or was the woman simply trying to catch the same bus? The passerby's attempt to play the hero had resulted in a strange and unresolved situation.

It highlighted the complexities and misunderstandings that can arise in our fast-paced, often chaotic world. Sometimes, what appears to be a clear-cut scenario may hold layers of untold stories and perspectives, reminding us that not everything is as it seems at first glance.

***

The 'Unexpected Turn' story illustrates how quick judgements can lead to misunderstandings. In life, we often encounter situations that are not what they initially appear to be. This tale encourages us to pause and reflect before acting, recognising the complexity of circumstances and the possibility of different perspectives. It reminds us that patience and open-mindedness are key to understanding the true nature of events and the people involved. Remember the Scottish Proverb, "Do not judge by appearances; a rich heart may be under a poor coat."

116. HAVING AN AIM

"The important thing in life is to have a great aim, and to possess the aptitude and the perseverance to attain it." – Goethe

Glenn Cunningham's journey began when he was 7 years old, facing a life-altering challenge. A severe burn injury left his legs so damaged that doctors contemplated amputation. However, in a twist of fate, they decided against it. One doctor, perhaps trying to set realistic expectations, suggested Glenn would eventually get used to sitting on a porch. But Glenn, with a determination that belied his age, firmly declared his intention not only to walk but to run.

Against all odds, 2 years later, Glenn was running. He wasn't the fastest, but he was defying every expectation. His running was more than just physical movement; it was a testament to his unyielding spirit. As he grew, his passion for running developed, becoming an integral part of his life. In college, he didn't just participate in track events; he excelled in them. Running transformed from a defiance of his fate to a pursuit of excellence.

Glenn's crowning moment came at the Berlin Olympics. It wasn't just about participating; it was about making history. Glenn not only qualified but shattered the Olympic record for the 1500-metre race. The boy who was once told he might never walk had now become the world's fastest human. His story wasn't just about physical recovery; it was a narrative of indomitable willpower, relentless perseverance, and the incredible capacity of the human spirit to overcome the gravest of adversities.

***

Glenn Cunningham's story is a powerful testament to human resilience and determination. It reminds us that limitations, whether physical or circumstantial, can be transcended with perseverance and courage. Glenn's journey from a near-impossible situation to becoming an Olympic record-breaker inspires us to confront challenges with resolve and hope. Let his story motivate you to defy odds, chase your dreams, and believe in the incredible potential that lies within each of us.

117. DEATH CANNOT BE EVADED

"It's not that I'm afraid to die. I just don't want to be there when it happens." – Woody Allen

In the lush gardens of a Persian palace, a prince strolled leisurely, accompanied by his loyal bodyguard. The tranquillity of the moment was abruptly interrupted when death appeared, casting a surprised glance at the bodyguard. Misinterpreting this as a sign of his imminent demise, the guard panicked. In a desperate attempt to escape his fate, he begged the prince for the fastest horse and fled towards his hometown, Tehran.

Meanwhile, the prince, puzzled by the encounter, later encountered death again within the palace walls. He questioned death about the unsettling incident in the garden. Death's response was both enlightening and chilling. "I did not intend to frighten him," death explained. "I was merely surprised to see him here when I was expecting him tonight in Tehran." The implication was clear and foreboding.

That night, in a twist of fate, the bodyguard, having reached Tehran, met his end – not because he fled, but because it was his destined time and place. This revelation left the prince deep in thought, contemplating the inescapable nature of destiny.

***

The tale of the Persian prince and his bodyguard teaches us a profound lesson about destiny and acceptance. It reminds us that certain aspects of life are predetermined, beyond our influence or control. Instead of living in fear or attempting to escape the inevitable, we should focus on embracing the present and living our lives to the fullest. Acceptance of our destiny allows us to find peace and purpose in the journey of life.

118. BURYING ONE'S TALENT

"The real tragedy of life is not in being limited to one talent, but in the failure to use the one talent." – Edgar W. Work

In a quaint village, there lived a miser who hoarded his wealth obsessively. His prized possession was a lump of gold, melted down from his vast fortune. Secretly, he buried it in a field, finding solace in visiting and gloating over his hidden treasure daily. The miser's life revolved around this ritual, providing him with a strange sense of comfort and security.

However, his secret was not to remain hidden. Servants in the village, having discovered the location of the gold, hatched a plan. One fateful night, under the veil of darkness, they unearthed the treasure and made away with it. The next morning, the miser, unaware of the night's events, made his usual pilgrimage to the field. Discovering the empty hole where his gold once lay, he was struck with inconsolable grief. His cries of despair echoed through the village, drawing the attention of his neighbours.

Among them was a wise friend who, upon hearing the miser's lament, offered a peculiar yet profound piece of advice. "Replace the gold with a brick," he suggested, "and continue your visits. You'll be no worse off than before, for you never used the gold anyway."

The friend's words were a stark revelation to the miser. His attachment to the gold had been purely psychological, offering him no practical benefit. This simple, yet eye-opening advice made the miser realise the folly of his ways. His wealth, never utilised, was as good as non-existent.

***

The story of the miser and his gold teaches a valuable lesson about the true worth of wealth. Hoarding riches without utilising them is akin to possessing nothing. This narrative encourages us to reflect on the way we value and use our resources. Wealth is only as valuable as its contribution to our lives and the lives of others. Let this tale be a reminder to invest our treasures, not just in the ground, but in enriching our experiences and helping others.

119. TO BE SOMEONE ELSE'S EYES

"The great poet is always a seer, seeing less with the eyes of the body than he does with the eyes of the mind."
– Oscar Wilde

In ancient Greece, the great poet Homer, already blind, was invited to a rich man's house to recite his poetry. Navigating with difficulty, Homer encountered a young boy, unaware that he was assisting the legendary bard. The boy, a slave in the rich man's household, revealed his plan to escape his bondage.

As they walked together, the boy guiding him, Homer felt a deep sense of gratitude. Upon reaching the house, Homer mesmerised the audience with his recital, captivating the rich man with his poetic brilliance. In a gesture of appreciation, the host offered Homer anything he desired from his wealth.

Contrary to expectations, Homer requested not gold or money, but the freedom of the slave boy. The rich man, moved by Homer's choice, agreed. As they left, Homer shared a profound thought with the boy, "From now on, you will be my eyes. Together, we can do a lot of good." This statement signified more than the physical aspect of sight; it was a bond of mutual support and a shared journey towards a greater purpose.

Homer's choice to liberate the boy over material wealth was a testament to his values. He saw in the boy not just a guide but a companion, someone who could help him navigate the world in a way he could not do alone.

***

Homer's story teaches us the value of human connection and the power of empathy. By choosing the boy's freedom over wealth, Homer showed that true wealth lies in relationships and helping others. This tale encourages us to look beyond our immediate needs and consider the impact we can have on others' lives. Let's remember that our greatest achievements often come from the support we offer and receive, creating a ripple effect of kindness and change.

120. THE UNSEEN BEAUTY WITHIN

"I can live for 2 months or a good compliment."
– Mark Twain

Joseph Lahey's story, as told in Guideposts magazine, begins with his childhood struggle with a crippled back. While his condition was less noticeable when clothed, the truth was starkly revealed whenever he was shirtless, leaving him feeling vulnerable and ashamed. This deep-seated self-consciousness reached a peak during a school health examination.

As Joseph nervously awaited his turn, the dread of exposing his back in front of the school doctor consumed him. His hands trembled as he untied his robe, revealing what he believed to be his greatest flaw. However, the doctor's reaction was unexpected and profound. Instead of focusing on his back, the doctor cupped Joseph's face, looked into his eyes, and asked if he believed in God. Upon Joseph's affirmative response, the doctor imparted a powerful message: "The more you believe in Him, the more you believe in yourself."

After a brief examination, the doctor stepped away, leaving Joseph alone with the medical chart. Curiosity overcoming him, Joseph inched forward to see what the doctor had written. To his surprise, under 'Physical Characteristics,' the note read: "Has an unusually well-shaped head." This simple, positive observation shifted Joseph's perception of himself.

The doctor's gesture and words were more than just a medical assessment; they were a lesson in seeing beyond physical imperfections. Joseph's story is a poignant reminder that beauty and worth are not just skin-deep but reside in how we view ourselves and what we choose to see in others.

***

Joseph Lahey's experience teaches us the importance of self-belief and seeing beyond physical imperfections. The doctor's focus on Joseph's well-shaped head, rather than his crippled back, highlights the value of recognising and appreciating our unique qualities. This story encourages us to look within and appreciate our inner beauty and strengths. Let us remember that our self-worth is not defined by external appearances but by the depth of our character and the goodness within us."

121. RESILIENCE AND HOPE

"Never cut down a tree in the wintertime. Never make a negative decision in a low time. Wait. Be patient. The spring will come." – Robert Schuller

Robert Schuller recounts a memorable winter at home when his father needed firewood. In search of a suitable tree, his father found one that appeared lifeless. It had no leaves, and its twigs snapped easily, a seemingly certain sign of its demise. With this belief, he sawed it down. However, as spring arrived, something unexpected happened. New shoots sprouted from the trunk of the fallen tree, defying all expectations of its death.

This surprising turn of events led to a profound reflection from Schuller's father. He shared with his son, "I thought sure it was dead; the leaves had dropped, the twigs snapped, it seemed as if there was no life there. But now, I see there is still life at the taproot of the old tree." This observation was followed by a valuable life lesson. He advised his son, "Bob, don't forget this important lesson. Never cut down a tree in wintertime. Never make a negative decision in a low time. Never make your most important decisions when you are in your worst mood. Wait. Be patient. The spring will come."

This story is a powerful metaphor for resilience and hope. It teaches us that even in the most barren and desolate phases of life, there remains a potential for revival and growth. It's a reminder to not hastily give up on situations or people during challenging times, as circumstances can change, bringing new beginnings and unexpected opportunities.

***

The story of the resilient winter tree teaches us the importance of patience and hope in difficult times. It reminds us that even in the bleakest moments, there's potential for growth and renewal. Before making significant decisions, especially in despair, it's crucial to wait and be patient, as circumstances can change. This narrative inspires us to believe in the 'spring' of life, a time of revival and new opportunities, encouraging us to hold onto hope and perseverance.

122. WORKING FOR PEACE

"Peace is a daily, a weekly, a monthly process, gradually changing opinions, slowly eroding old barriers, quietly building new structures." – John F. Kennedy

In August 1985, tragedy struck when a plane crash claimed the life of 13-year-old American girl Samantha Smith. But her short life had already made a profound impact. A few years prior, Samantha had become an international symbol of peace. Her journey began one morning when she read about the arms race in a newspaper. Fearful of a nuclear war between the United States and the Soviet Union, she did something extraordinary for a child: she wrote a letter to Yuri Andropov, the Soviet leader.

Samantha expressed her fears candidly: "I am worried about Russia and America getting into a nuclear war. It scares me to death! Are you going for war? Please tell me how we can stop a war." Remarkably, Andropov responded, inviting her to visit Russia. In 1983, accompanied by her parents, Samantha travelled to the Soviet Union. There, she met Russian children her age, forging friendships that transcended political boundaries.

Upon returning to America, Samantha shared her insights: "If we can be friends by getting to know each other better, then what are our 2 countries arguing about? Nothing could be more important than stopping a nuclear war." Samantha's simple, yet profound message resonated globally. She became a symbol of hope, advocating for peace and understanding between 2 superpowers during a time of heightened tension.

***

Samantha Smith's story is a testament to the power of one young voice to bridge divides, inspire dialogue, and remind the world of the importance of striving for peace. Her courageous act of reaching out to a world leader showed that empathy, dialogue, and understanding are key to resolving conflicts. Her legacy teaches us that peace begins with open communication and the willingness to see beyond our differences. Let her memory inspire us to foster peace and unity in our own lives and communities.

123. PEACE AMIDST THE STORM

"Peace is not the absence of turmoil but the presence of calm in the heart of it." – Unknown

Long ago, a man sought the perfect representation of peace. Dissatisfied with existing depictions, he announced a contest to find this ideal image. Artists from all corners were inspired, sending their works in anticipation of the grand reveal. The day of judgement arrived, and the event unfolded with great excitement. One by one, serene scenes were unveiled, each earning applause and admiration. The atmosphere brimmed with tension as only 2 paintings remained covered.

The first revealed painting depicted a tranquil scene: a mirror-smooth lake reflecting the soft hues of the evening sky, and a flock of sheep grazing peacefully along the grassy shore. The audience was certain this was the embodiment of peace.

However, the unveiling of the second painting brought a wave of surprise. It depicted a tumultuous waterfall cascading down a rocky cliff, with storm clouds ready to burst, and a chilling wind that seemed to leap out of the canvas. In this chaotic scene, a slender tree clung precariously to the rocks, its branch extending towards the waterfall. Nestled in this branch was a small bird, calmly resting on her eggs, unaffected by the surrounding turmoil.

This contrasting image of calm amidst chaos captured the essence of true peace. The little bird, undisturbed in her stormy environment, symbolised peace that transcends external disturbances. This profound depiction reminded the observers that peace is not merely the absence of conflict or noise, but a serene inner state that persists even in the midst of life's storms.

***

The story of the perfect picture of peace teaches us that true peace is found within, amidst life's tumultuous situations. The serene bird in the stormy painting symbolises inner tranquillity that endures regardless of external circumstances. This tale encourages us to cultivate such peace within ourselves, remaining calm and centred in the face of life's challenges. True peace is an internal sanctuary, unaffected by the chaos of the world, a haven we carry within us.

124. BUILD WITH BEST BRICKS

"Integrity is doing the right thing, even when no one is watching." – C.S. Lewis

An elderly contractor, nearing retirement, was presented with one final project by an engineer. This project, a grand palace, was to be a testament to his years of workmanship. Granted the liberty to use the finest materials, the contractor faced a pivotal choice. Tempted by the prospect of lucrative gain, he opted for a path that strayed from his usual dedication to quality. Instead of pouring his heart and soul into the work, he resorted to shoddy workmanship, using inferior materials to cut costs and maximise his profit. This decision marked a departure from the integrity that had characterised his career.

The palace, completed with superficial grandeur, was unveiled amidst a celebration. Friends and well-wishers gathered, admiring the outward splendour of the construction. During the inaugural function, the engineer delivered an unexpected announcement. He proclaimed that the palace was to be gifted to the contractor as a token of gratitude for his 25 years of service. This revelation struck the contractor with profound regret. If he had known he was building his own house, he lamented, he would have approached the task differently.

***

The story of the elderly contractor teaches a crucial lesson about integrity and foresight. It reminds us to uphold our values and standards in all we do, as our actions invariably come back to us. The regret of the contractor highlights the importance of treating every task as if it were for our own benefit. Let this story be a call to consistently practise integrity and excellence, knowing that the work we do is ultimately a reflection of ourselves.

125. A MARATHON OF HOPE

"All about me may be silence and darkness, yet within me, in the spirit, is music and brightness, and colour flashes through all my thoughts." – Helen Keller

Terry Fox, a 22-year-old student at Simon Fraser University in Canada, faced a life-altering challenge in 1977. Diagnosed with bone cancer, he underwent the amputation of his right leg. Despite this devastating setback, Terry's spirit remained unbroken. His resilience was further ignited by a newspaper article about a handicapped person running in a New York marathon, sent by his high school basketball coach.

Inspired, Terry set a monumental goal. He aimed to run across Canada, a staggering distance of 5,000 miles, to raise funds for cancer research. For 18 months, he trained relentlessly on his artificial leg, a testament to his extraordinary determination.

On April 12, 1980, Terry embarked on his "Marathon of Hope," with over a million dollars in sponsorship. His journey captured the hearts of the nation. Braving pain and exhaustion, Terry ran an average of 26 miles a day. However, after 3,000 miles and 114 days, tragedy struck. Terry collapsed; the cancer had metastasised to his lungs.

As news of Terry's condition spread, a remarkable wave of support ensued. Canadians, moved by his courage, donated generously. Within hours, over $24 million was raised for cancer research. Though Terry passed away a few days later, his legacy endured.

Terry Fox's Marathon of Hope stands as a powerful symbol of perseverance, selflessness, and the human capacity to turn personal tragedy into a collective triumph for a greater cause.

***

Terry Fox's remarkable journey exemplifies unwavering determination and hope in the face of adversity. His Marathon of Hope, though cut short, sparked a movement that continues to inspire and raise funds for cancer research. Terry's story teaches us that one person's courage can ignite a nation's spirit and drive meaningful change. Let his legacy remind us to face challenges with bravery and to transform personal struggles into opportunities for communal upliftment and progress.

126. PUTTING THE WORLD RIGHT

"When we strive to become better than we are, everything around us becomes better, too." – Paulo Coelho

A father returned home one day with a unique challenge for his son. He presented a torn-up map of the world and asked his young son to piece it back together. Expecting this task to be beyond the boy's grasp, the father was astounded when, in just 10 minutes, the boy returned with the map perfectly restored.

The father's curiosity was piqued. How had his son, with little knowledge of geography, managed such a feat in record time? Upon inquiry, the boy's explanation was both simple and profound. "All I did was to put the man right, and the world came out right." It turned out that on the reverse side of the map was a picture of a man. By focusing on aligning the human figure, the boy inadvertently aligned the world map on the other side.

***

This story illustrates a profound truth about our world and our role in it. The child's approach to the task highlights a fundamental insight: when we focus on improving ourselves, on 'putting the man right,' we can inadvertently contribute to 'putting the world right.' The story underscores the importance of personal growth and introspection as a pathway to broader societal change. Personal growth and integrity are not just self-serving pursuits but are integral to creating a harmonious and balanced world.

127. NO ONE DESERVES MERCY!

"Blessed are the merciful; for they shall obtain mercy."
– Matthew 5:7

In the era of Napoleon's army, a young French soldier committed a grave act of desertion. Quickly captured by his own troops, he faced the inevitable consequence of his decision: the death penalty. This harsh rule was enforced to deter soldiers from abandoning their posts, a critical measure in maintaining the army's discipline and effectiveness.

News of the soldier's fate reached his mother, who was gripped by a desperate resolve to save her son. She journeyed to meet Napoleon, hoping to sway the emperor's heart with her plea. Upon reaching him, she presented her case, imploring for mercy for her son. Napoleon, unmoved, pointed out the severity of the soldier's crime, emphasising that he did not deserve mercy.

The mother's response to Napoleon's assertion was both poignant and insightful. "I know he doesn't deserve mercy," she admitted. "It wouldn't be mercy if he deserved it." This simple yet profound statement struck at the very essence of mercy: it is an act of compassion and forgiveness extended particularly when it is least deserved.

***

The story of the young soldier and his mother teaches us about the true essence of mercy. It reminds us that mercy is not about giving someone what they deserve, but offering compassion and forgiveness even when it's least expected. This narrative encourages us to practice mercy in our own lives, understanding that it can be a powerful force for change and redemption. Let's embrace the spirit of grace, extending kindness and forgiveness, even in challenging situations.

128. CARING FOR THE WORLD

"One who plants trees, knowing that he will never sit in their shade, has at least started to understand the meaning of life." – Rabindranath Tagore

This is a tale of a young explorer venturing into the Alpine mountains. There, he encountered an old man engaged in an unusual task. The man was methodically planting acorns with an iron staff across a barren stretch of land. Intrigued, the explorer learned that the old man had already planted over a thousand seeds, with a steadfast commitment to reforest an area left desolate.

The explorer, sceptical of the old man's efforts, saw it as a futile pursuit, an investment unlikely to bear fruit in his lifetime. He laughed at what seemed like a wasted endeavour, unable to grasp the vision that drove the old man's actions.

Three decades later, the explorer, now a matured man, returned to the same location. To his astonishment, the desolate land had transformed into a thriving oak forest, spanning 11 kilometres in length and 3 kilometres in width. The area was a symphony of life: birds singing in the boughs, sweet-scented flowers perfuming the air, wildlife frolicking in the cool shade, and streams flowing through what were once parched groves.

This transformation was a testament to the old man's vision and perseverance. His solitary work had turned a barren land into a flourishing ecosystem. The explorer's initial mockery turned into profound admiration and respect. He realised that the old man's seemingly small, consistent efforts had a monumental impact, creating a legacy that would endure for generations.

***

The story of the old man and the oak forest is a profound lesson in vision and perseverance. It shows us that even the smallest, consistent efforts can lead to significant change over time. The transformation of a barren land into a thriving forest symbolises the power of hope and dedication in overcoming seemingly insurmountable challenges. Let this story inspire us to commit to our goals, understanding that patience and persistence can yield extraordinary results, often beyond our initial expectations.

129. THE GIRAFFE'S FIRST LESSON

"Life's challenges are not supposed to paralyse you; they're supposed to help you discover who you are."
– Bernice Johnson Reagon

In the wild, a mother giraffe presents her newborn with a startling introduction to life. Upon giving birth, the baby giraffe falls from its mother's womb, landing on the hard ground. This sudden transition from warmth and security to the harsh realities of the jungle is just the beginning. The mother giraffe, instead of coddling her offspring, takes an unexpected approach. She gets behind the baby and delivers a hard kick, forcing it to its feet.

The baby, with weak and wobbly legs, struggles to stand and quickly falls. Undeterred, the mother continues her seemingly harsh treatment, kicking the baby again. This cycle repeats several times. With each kick, the baby's strength grows; it learns to steady itself, eventually standing firm and starting to move.

This peculiar method of mothering is driven by a vital instinct: in the jungle, a baby giraffe's survival depends on its ability to stand and move quickly to avoid predators. The mother's kicks, though seemingly harsh, are acts of love. They are critical lessons in resilience and self-reliance, teaching the young giraffe to rise swiftly in the face of adversity.

***

The giraffe's first lesson teaches us about resilience and the importance of facing challenges head-on. The mother giraffe's tough love approach is a metaphor for life's hardships, reminding us that struggles often prepare us for survival. This story inspires us to embrace challenges, recognising them as opportunities for growth and strength. Let us learn from the giraffe: to get up quickly when we fall and to understand that sometimes, the hardest lessons are the most valuable.

130. SELF-DISCIPLINE

"Children are educated by what the grown-up is and not by his talk." – Carl Jung

A man was haunted by a vivid dream. In it, he saw his teenage son playing joyously in an open field with peers. Abruptly, the scene shifted. The boy wandered into a dark by-lane, disappearing from sight. Panicked, the father called out, 'Son, where are you going?' As the distance grew, the son glanced back, his words striking like a thunderbolt, 'Dad! You never showed me the right path to follow.' Jolted awake, the father sat up, a cold sweat drenching his skin.

This dream was more than a fleeting nightmare; it was a wake-up call. Reflecting on his life, the father recognised the unsettling truth. Engrossed in his own world, he had neglected his role as a guide and role model for his son. His actions, or rather the lack thereof, had left his son without a beacon to navigate life's complexities.

Consumed by this realisation, the father decided to transform his life. He resolved to be more present, engaged, and to lead by example. He committed to showing his son the values of integrity, hard work, and compassion through his own actions. The father understood that mere words were not enough; it was through his deeds that he would illuminate the path for his son.

***

The story of the father's transformative dream highlights the crucial role of parents as guides and role models. It reminds us that our actions speak louder than words in teaching our children life's important lessons. Let this story inspire parents to lead by example, showing their children the way through their own actions and choices. By being present, engaged, and exemplary in our behaviour, we can light the path for our children to follow, shaping their futures positively.

131. PARENTAL INFLUENCE

"Too much love never spoils children. Children become spoiled when we substitute 'presents' for 'presence.'"
– Anthony Witham

Once, there lived a little boy, the only son of his parents, who received everything he desired. From infancy, he was coddled, and never denied anything. His first birthday gift was a toy gun, and whenever he cried, he was instantly comforted. His parents believed that letting him cry or denying his wishes would mean not loving him enough.

As the boy grew, he was never disciplined. He could leave the house anytime, break window panes, knock down flowerpots, and face no consequences. His parents thought that stifling his will would be unloving. The mother did all his chores, fearing that asking him to help would be interpreted as a lack of love. Even when he used bad words or scribbled on walls, he was not reprimanded, as his creativity was not to be stifled.

The boy never attended religion classes or learned about God and His creation. His parents didn't want to force religion upon him, equating it to not loving him. However, this path of unchecked freedom and lack of guidance led to a tragic turn. One day, the parents received news that their son was in jail on criminal charges. Devastated, they couldn't comprehend where they went wrong, lamenting, "All we ever did was love him and make sure he never got hurt…"

***

The story of the little boy and his parents teaches the importance of balance in love and discipline. It illustrates how overindulgence and the absence of boundaries, under the guise of love, can lead to adverse outcomes. This narrative reminds us that true love involves guidance, setting limits, and teaching responsibility. It's a call to understand that loving someone also means preparing them for the real world, where actions have consequences, and discipline is key to growth.

132. CORRECT UPBRINGING

"It is the function of parents to see that their children habitually experience the true consequences of their conduct." – Herbert Spencer

A young boy's journey to a life of crime began with a seemingly minor transgression. He stole an instrument box from a school companion and brought it home. His mother, upon discovering the theft, chose not to discipline him. Instead, she praised his cunning, reinforcing his belief that such acts were not only acceptable but commendable.

Encouraged by his mother's approval, the boy's criminal behaviour escalated as he grew older. His thefts grew more audacious and valuable, culminating in his eventual arrest for a significant crime. Tried and convicted, he was sentenced to death.

On the day of his execution, a crowd gathered to witness his final walk to the gallows. Among them was his mother, now overcome with grief and wailing in despair. The boy requested to speak to her one last time. As she leaned in, expecting perhaps a word of love or regret, he did something shocking: he bit off her ear. The crowd, horrified, condemned this final act of brutality.

Yet, the boy's response to their outrage revealed a deeper truth. He explained that his mother's failure to discipline him for his initial theft set him on this destructive path.

Had she corrected him then, he argued, his life would have taken a different turn.

***

The story of the boy and his mother highlights the critical role of discipline and guidance in a child's upbringing. It serves as a cautionary tale about the consequences of indulgence and the lack of accountability. This narrative reminds us that true love and care involve teaching children right from wrong and preparing them for the moral complexities of life. Let it be a reminder to embrace our responsibilities in shaping young lives with wisdom, love, and appropriate boundaries.

133. MAKING AMENDS

"Every man ought to have the chance to correct his epitaph in midstream and write a new one." - Alfred Nobel

Alfred Nobel, the inventor of dynamite, experienced a profound moment that altered his legacy. One morning, he woke up to read his own obituary in the local newspaper. It was a case of mistaken identity; the obituary was meant for his brother. However, the impact of reading his supposed legacy was life-changing. The obituary labelled him as the man "who devised a way for more people to be killed in a war than ever before" and died wealthy because of it.

This unsettling portrayal deeply troubled Nobel. He was dismayed to realise that, had he been the one to die, his memory would have been tied to destruction and death. This realisation struck a chord in Nobel's conscience. He was grieved by the thought of being remembered only for contributing to warfare and amassing a fortune through such means.

Driven by this eye-opening experience, Nobel resolved to redefine his legacy. He sought to transform his image from a harbinger of death to a benefactor of humanity. This led to the inception of the Nobel Prize, an award honouring those whose contributions significantly benefit society. Nobel's statement, "Every man ought to have the chance to correct his epitaph in midstream and write a new one," reflected his desire for redemption and positive impact.

***

Alfred Nobel's story teaches us the importance of legacy and the power of self-reflection. His experience of reading his own mistaken obituary led him to profoundly change the way he would be remembered. This narrative reminds us that it's never too late to redefine our contributions to the world. Let Nobel's transformation inspire us to consider the impact of our actions and to strive for a legacy that positively affects humanity and leaves a lasting, beneficial imprint.

134. MAKING A DIFFERENCE

"We cannot do great things on this Earth, only small things with great love." – Mother Teresa

On a Mexican beach, 2 men strolled along the shore, deep in conversation. In the distance, they noticed a figure repeatedly bending down and throwing something into the ocean. As they approached, it became clear that the figure was a local native, engaged in a curious activity.

The beach was littered with starfish, left stranded by the outgoing tide. The native was diligently picking up each starfish and hurling it back into the sea. Intrigued, one of the men asked, "What are you doing?" The native replied, "I am throwing the starfish back out to sea. If they don't get back into deeper water, they will die."

The man acknowledged this but then pointed out the vast number of starfish on the beach. "There are thousands stranded out here," he said. "How do you feel that this will make a difference?" The beach seemed endless, and the task at hand, insurmountable.

Undeterred, the native bent over, picked up another starfish, and threw it into the ocean. With a smile, he responded, "Made a difference to that one!" His simple yet profound action and words echoed a powerful message.

***

The Starfish Thrower story teaches us about the significance of individual actions in making a difference. It reminds us that even in seemingly hopeless situations, our efforts can have a meaningful impact, even if it's just for one. This tale inspires us to not be discouraged by the magnitude of a challenge but to focus on the difference we can make. Let's be motivated to take action, understanding that every small act of kindness contributes to a greater good.

135. THE SILENT ACCUSATION

"Out of suffering have emerged the strongest souls; the most massive characters are seared with scars." – Kahlil Gibran

Kahlil Gibran's story "The Forerunner" begins with a traveller arriving at an inn at dusk. Trusting the safety of the place, he ties his horse to a tree beside the door and enters the inn. However, by midnight, a thief steals his horse. The next morning, upon discovering the theft, his fellow lodgers surround him with a barrage of criticisms.

One lodger chides the traveller for tying his horse outside instead of in the stable, while another rebukes him for not fettering the horse. A third comments on the foolishness of travelling by sea on horseback, and a fourth critiques the laziness implied by owning a horse.

The traveller, overwhelmed by these unsolicited opinions, is astonished. In a moment of realisation, he exclaims, "My friends, because my horse is stolen, you have hastened to tell me my faults and shortcomings. But strangely, not a word of reproach you have uttered about the man who stole my horse."

***

The story 'The Silent Accusation' by Kahlil Gibran teaches us about empathy and perspective in the face of misfortune. It reminds us that in times of adversity, we should offer support rather than criticism. The traveller's experience encourages us to focus on the injustice committed, rather than scrutinising the victim's actions. This tale urges us to be mindful and empathetic, offering constructive help instead of judgement, and understanding instead of blame, in our interactions with others.

136. BEING TRUTHFUL

"Truth never damages a cause that is just." – Mahatma Gandhi

As a young boy, Mohandas Karamchand Gandhi, who would later be known as Mahatma Gandhi, faced a situation that would be a defining moment in his life. In his school, it was announced that the Inspector of Schools would visit. Anticipating this, the teacher, eager to make a good impression, intensely tutored the children.

On the day of the inspection, as the Inspector made his rounds, he decided to test the students on their spelling. He asked them to spell 'kettle.' Many students raised their hands, but the Inspector specifically called upon young Mohandas. Confused, Mohandas spelled the word incorrectly. In a bid to save face for the school, the teacher discreetly prompted Mohandas with the correct spelling.

However, young Gandhi, standing firm in his principles, refused to heed the teacher's whispers. He chose to stand by his original answer, despite knowing it was incorrect. This act of refusing to cheat, even under pressure and in a seemingly inconsequential situation, was a testament to his strong character.

***

The story of young Gandhi's refusal to cheat on a spelling test teaches us the importance of integrity and honesty. It illustrates that even small acts of truthfulness are significant and shape our character. This narrative inspires us to adhere to our principles, regardless of external pressures or temptations. Let Gandhi's childhood example remind us that true greatness lies in our commitment to honesty and integrity, even in seemingly minor aspects of our lives.

137. GOING THROUGH PAST RECORDS

"We live in the present, we dream of the future, but we learn eternal truths from the past." – Madam Chiang Kai-shek

Jack and Merlin's 20 years of marriage had reached a breaking point. Convinced that their relationship was beyond repair, they decided to part ways. As Jack sorted through their financial accounts to ensure an amicable divorce, he stumbled upon old chequebooks that held more than just records of transactions.

Each cancelled cheque he encountered was a tangible piece of their shared history. The first cheque brought back memories of their honeymoon, a time of love and new beginnings. The second was for their first car, a symbol of their journey together. The third reminded him of the birth of their daughter, a milestone that deepened their bond. And the fourth, for Rs. 200,000, represented their first home, a testament to their commitment and shared dreams.

Overwhelmed by these reminders of their intertwined lives, Jack's resolve wavered. He realised that their marriage was not just a legal union but a tapestry of shared experiences and memories. Pushing the chequebooks aside, he reached for the phone and called Merlin. His voice, imbued with emotion, conveyed a simple yet profound message: they had invested too much in each other to let it go so easily.

This phone call marked the beginning of a new chapter. Through open communication and a renewed appreciation for their shared past, Jack and Merlin found a way to rekindle the love and harmony that had once defined their home.

***

Jack and Merlin's story illustrates the power of reflection and the enduring impact of shared experiences in relationships. It reminds us that sometimes, looking back at the journey together can reignite the spark that seems lost. This narrative encourages couples to value their shared history and to consider the depth of their investment in each other before parting ways. Let their story inspire a reevaluation of relationships, fostering reconciliation, and a renewed commitment to cherish and nurture the bond.

138. DOING WORTHWHILE THINGS

"Love begins by taking care of the closest ones – the ones at home." – Mother Teresa

A well-to-do twenty-year-old university student from West Bengal experienced a transformative moment that reshaped his outlook on life. Escaping college to catch a movie with friends, his path unexpectedly crossed with Mother Teresa, though he didn't recognise her at the time. She beckoned him for help with a task that would challenge his very being.

Mother Teresa, in her white sari, needed assistance with a half-dead man sprawled over a garbage heap, his body decomposing and emitting a foul stench. Despite his initial horror, the student was captivated by the nun's compassionate demeanour. Almost in a trance, he found himself helping her, his actions driven by a force he couldn't explain.

Compelled by a newfound sense of purpose, the student joined Mother Teresa in the ambulance, accompanying them to the home. There, he knelt and washed the dying man's sore-covered feet. This act, though small in the grand scheme of things, was monumental for him. He felt, perhaps for the first time, that he was partaking in a genuinely worthwhile act, one that transcended his own life and touched another's in their final moments.

This chance encounter was more than just an act of kindness; it was a profound lesson in empathy, compassion, and the impact one individual can have on another. The student's experience with Mother Teresa opened his eyes to a world of suffering and the power of selfless service, leaving an indelible mark on his heart and mind.

***

The story of the young man's encounter with Mother Teresa highlights the profound impact of compassion and service to others. It reminds us that stepping out of our comfort zones to help those in need can be a deeply transformative experience. This narrative encourages us to look beyond our own lives and engage in acts of kindness and empathy. Let this story inspire us to embrace opportunities for service, understanding the profound fulfilment and perspective that comes from helping others in need.

139. SHOWING EMPATHY

"Pity is feeling sorry for someone; empathy is feeling sorry with someone." – Martin Luther King, Jr

In a small pet store, a boy discovered a group of puppies for sale, each priced at $49. Among them, separated and alone, was a puppy without a price tag. Curious, the boy inquired about its absence. The store owner explained that the puppy was born with a missing leg and lacked a hip socket, rendering it deformed.

The boy, moved by the puppy's plight, asked to play with it. As he lifted the puppy, it affectionately licked his ear, instantly forming a bond. The boy, determined to purchase this particular puppy, offered $49. The store owner, perplexed, questioned why the boy would choose the handicapped puppy over a healthy one for the same price. Without a word, the boy lifted his left trouser leg, revealing an artificial leg.

This silent revelation spoke volumes. It was a moment of profound understanding between the boy and the store owner. The boy saw himself as the puppy, a creature facing the world with a physical challenge, yet full of life and love. The store owner, recognising this unspoken bond, quietly agreed to the sale.

***

The story of the boy and the handicapped puppy teaches us about empathy and the deep connections formed through shared experiences. It illustrates how understanding and compassion can bridge differences, fostering special bonds. This narrative encourages us to look beyond the surface and appreciate the unique qualities of others, regardless of their imperfections. Let this story inspire us to form meaningful relationships based on empathy and mutual understanding, recognising the value and beauty in all beings.

140. CONSEQUENCES OF BAD EXAMPLE

"Children have never been very good at listening to their elders, but they have never failed to imitate them." – James Baldwin

Twelve-year-old Tommy witnessed 2 defining moments with his parents, each leaving a lasting impression. The first incident occurred with his father, who was speeding when stopped by a patrol officer. Instead of accepting the consequences, Tommy's father casually bribed the officer with a 50 rupee note. As the officer smiled and let them go, his father turned to Tommy and justified his action, saying, "Everybody does it, you know."

The second incident involved Tommy's mother. While shopping at a cosmetic store, the cashier mistakenly handed her extra money. Without hesitation, she slipped the excess cash into her handbag. Turning to Tommy, she echoed a similar justification as his father, "Everybody does it, you know."

These experiences taught Tommy a skewed view of morality and ethics, guided by the principle that the end justifies the means if "everybody does it." The culmination of these lessons came when Tommy was caught cheating in an examination. When confronted by his shocked parents about his dishonesty, Tommy, feeling justified, retorted with the same rationale he had learned from them, "Dad! Mum! Everybody does it, you know!"

***

Tommy's story illustrates the powerful influence parents have on shaping their children's moral compass. It serves as a cautionary tale about the consequences of justifying unethical behaviour with the notion that 'everybody does it.' This narrative encourages parents and guardians to be mindful of the examples they set, understanding that children often emulate their actions. Let this story be a reminder to uphold integrity and teach children the importance of honesty and ethical behaviour in all aspects of life.

141. ATTAINING THE GOAL

"Life isn't about finding yourself. Life is about creating yourself." – George Bernard Shaw

George Bernard Shaw, a renowned playwright, had encounters with many influential individuals throughout his life, including poets, authors, dramatists, and actors. These interactions presented him with unique perspectives and opportunities for self-reflection. One day, a close friend posed a thought-provoking question to Shaw: "Bernard, in your life, you have met many famous people. If you were to live your life again, which of them would you like to be?"

Shaw's response to this query was as insightful as it was unexpected. He said, "I would like to be the person; George Bernard Shaw could have been but never was." This profound statement reflected a deep sense of self-awareness and contemplation about his own life and potential. It wasn't a wish to be someone else but a desire to fulfil his own unmet potential.

This response reveals an introspective understanding that, despite his success and fame, he believed he had not achieved his fullest potential. Shaw recognised that every individual, regardless of their accomplishments, harbours the capacity to achieve more, to push boundaries further, and to explore uncharted territories within themselves.

***

George Bernard Shaw's response about his life's aspirations teaches us about recognising and striving for our unfulfilled potential. It reminds us that no matter our achievements, there is always room for growth and improvement. This story inspires us to reflect on our own lives, encouraging us to pursue our fullest potential and not settle for what we have achieved so far. Let's embrace the idea of continuous self-improvement, aspiring to be the best versions of ourselves.

142. SPREADING RUMOURS

"Never believe anything bad about anybody unless you feel that it is absolutely necessary – and that God is listening while you tell it." – Henry Van Dyke

In a school, a teacher approached the principal with the intention of sharing something she had heard. Anticipating a typical exchange of information, she was taken aback by the principal's unexpected response. The principal posed 3 critical questions: "Is it true? Will it be useful to me? Will it bring some humour?"

The teacher, pondering these questions, realised that what she intended to share did not meet any of these criteria. It wasn't a verified truth, nor was it particularly useful or light-hearted. The principal's insightful questions led to an epiphany for the teacher. She understood that the information she was about to pass on was mere hearsay, lacking in substance and value.

The principal's approach to communication was a profound lesson in mindfulness and responsibility. By asking these questions, he encouraged the teacher to reflect on the nature and purpose of what she was sharing. His approach emphasised the importance of thoughtful communication, discouraging the spread of rumours or unverified information.

***

The story of the teacher and the principal teaches the importance of mindful communication. It emphasises the value of sharing information that is true, useful, or positive. This narrative encourages us to reflect on the impact of our words and to choose our conversations wisely. Let this story be a reminder to engage in meaningful communication, contributing positively to our surroundings and discouraging the spread of unverified or harmful information.

143. PROUD WINNERS

"Alone we can do so little; together we can do so much."
– Helen Keller

In a Special Olympics event, a heartwarming scene unfolded during the 100-metre dash. Nine children, each with their unique challenges, lined up at the start line, their faces alight with excitement and determination. As the starting gun sounded, they burst forward with enthusiasm. But mere yards into the race, one of the children stumbled and fell, his cries piercing the air.

In a typical race, the competitors would have seized this moment to surge ahead. However, these children, unbound by conventional notions of competition and rivalry, reacted differently. The remaining 8 runners stopped in their tracks. They turned back, their concern overriding their desire to win.

Together, they helped their fallen comrade to his feet. What happened next was a beautiful display of unity and compassion. The children, arm in arm, ran together towards the finish line. Their collective action transformed the race from a competition into a celebration of solidarity and empathy.

The audience, witnessing this extraordinary moment, rose to their feet in a standing ovation. The applause that echoed through the stadium was not for a single victor but for all 9 children. Each runner had shown that winning isn't always about crossing the finish line first; sometimes, it's about ensuring everyone makes it to the end together.

***

The Special Olympics race story exemplifies the essence of unity and compassion over competition. It teaches us that true victory lies in helping others and achieving goals together. This tale inspires us to value cooperation and empathy, understanding that success is not always about individual achievement but also about lifting each other up. Let this story be a reminder to embrace the spirit of togetherness and celebrate collective accomplishments, reinforcing the notion that everyone wins when we support one another.

144. IN SEARCH OF DIAMONDS

"Happiness is not in the mere possession of money; it lies in the joy of achievement, in the thrill of creative effort." – Franklin D. Roosevelt

The story of Ali Facid, a farmer, unfolds with a visit from a Buddhist priest who spoke of the wealth that diamonds could bring. Intrigued and restless, Ali Facid's peaceful life was disrupted by the relentless pursuit of this newfound dream. The thought of diamonds and the wealth they promised haunted him, leading him to a drastic decision.

Consumed by the desire for riches, Ali Facid sold his farm, left his family with neighbours, and embarked on a quest to find diamonds. His journey was long and arduous, taking him far from home. Months turned into years, and Ali Facid's search proved futile. His health deteriorated, his spirit broke, and his funds depleted. In a tragic twist of fate, overwhelmed by despair and exhaustion, he ended his life in the Bay of Barcelona.

Meanwhile, back at his former farm, the new owner discovered a surprising truth. One day, while working the land, he found a stone that shone with an unusual brilliance. It was a diamond, hidden right under the surface of the farm. Further exploration revealed that the farm was rich with diamonds, acres of them lying just beneath the surface.

***

The tale of Ali Facid and his quest for diamonds teaches us about the value of contentment and the dangers of relentless ambition. It serves as a reminder to appreciate what we have, recognising that often, the greatest treasures are found within our reach. This story encourages us to seek happiness and fulfilment in our current circumstances, understanding that the pursuit of distant dreams can sometimes blind us to the real wealth that lies close to home.

145. HANDLING ADVERSITY

"Adversity can be our greatest motivation for spiritual growth or our deadliest means of discouragement." – John Bevere

In a quiet countryside, a farmer's donkey fell into an abandoned well. The distressed animal brayed pitifully as the farmer pondered over the situation. Concluding that the donkey was old and rescuing it would be too cumbersome, he made a difficult decision. He decided to bury the donkey in the well, rationalising that the well needed to be covered anyway.

The farmer called his neighbours to assist him, and they began to shovel dirt into the well. As the dirt rained down on the donkey's back, a remarkable transformation occurred. Instead of succumbing to despair, the donkey shook off each shovel of dirt and stepped up onto the new layer of soil. This process repeated with every shovel of dirt: shake off and step up.

The farmer and his neighbours watched in disbelief as the donkey, instead of being buried, gradually ascended toward the well's opening. With each shovel of dirt, the donkey rose higher. Eventually, to everyone's astonishment, the donkey stepped over the edge of the well and trotted off, free from the pit that was meant to be its grave.

***

The story of the donkey in the well teaches us the power of resilience in the face of adversity. It illustrates how we can turn seemingly insurmountable challenges into opportunities to rise stronger. This tale encourages us to 'shake off' our troubles and take a step up, reminding us that it's not the nature of the challenge that defines us but how we respond to it. Let this story inspire us to face obstacles with courage and determination.

146. DEDICATION TO DUTY

"The measure of a man is the way he bears up under misfortune." – Plutarch

Sardar Patel, known as the 'Iron Man of India,' was recognised for his remarkable composure in times of crisis. Before joining India's Freedom Movement under Mahatma Gandhi's leadership, he was a successful lawyer. One day, while deeply engrossed in arguing a case before a judge, Patel received a telegram. Without any visible disturbance, he calmly read the message, placed it in his pocket, and continued his argument with unwavering focus.

After the hearing concluded, the judge, curious about the telegram's content, approached Patel. Patel revealed that the telegram had informed him of his wife's death. The judge expressed his condolences and admiration for Patel's extraordinary dedication to his professional duty. This incident highlighted Patel's exceptional ability to maintain his composure and focus, even in the face of personal tragedy.

Patel's reaction was not one of indifference but a demonstration of practical wisdom. He understood that his wife's passing was irreversible and chose not to let his emotions overwhelm him at that moment. Instead, he focused entirely on defending his client, embodying a profound sense of responsibility and professionalism.

***

Sardar Patel's response to receiving tragic news during a court case exemplifies remarkable composure and dedication to duty. His ability to continue his professional responsibilities amidst personal grief teaches us about resilience and the importance of focus. This story inspires us to handle life's challenges with grace and determination, balancing personal emotions with professional obligations. Let us learn from Patel's example the value of maintaining our composure and dedication, even in the most trying circumstances.

147. NO FREE LUNCH

"There ain't no such thing as a free lunch." – Economist Milton Friedman

Once there was a King who wished to pass on the hard-earned wisdom of the ages to future generations. He commanded his learned advisers to distil all they knew into writings that would stand the test of time.

The advisers laboured long, producing many lengthy volumes. But the King found them too dense for ordinary folk to grasp. "Simplify the message," he ordered. Again and again, they reduced the writings – first to one book, then a chapter, then a single page – but still the King was unsatisfied. Finally, the advisers captured the essence in one pithy sentence: "There is no free lunch."

At last, the King was pleased. Though all knowledge could not be handed down for free, this single kernel would inspire future seekers of wisdom to work for true understanding. For wisdom, like all worthy things, comes at a price.

***

The final wisdom, 'There is no free lunch,' highlights that nothing valuable comes without effort or a price. True wisdom is earned through long effort and cannot simply be passed on. We must each seek our path to insight, not expect enlightenment to be handed to us. The rewards of wisdom only come to those willing to work and sacrifice.

148. THE REALITY OF LONELINESS

"Kindness is the language which the deaf can hear and the blind can see." – Mark Twain

Once, the esteemed poet Rupert Brooke embarked on a journey from England to America. Amidst the bustling crowd on the dock, everyone seemed to have loved ones bidding them farewell, everyone except Rupert. He watched enviously as others shared embraces and tearful goodbyes, feeling a deep sense of loneliness.

In the midst of his solitude, Rupert's eyes landed on a young boy standing alone. Approaching him, Rupert asked his name. "William," the boy replied. Seizing an opportunity, Rupert offered, "William, would you like to earn a few shillings?" Intrigued, William eagerly agreed. Rupert's request was simple yet profound, "Just wave to me as I leave."

As the ship began to depart, the scene on the dock was a tapestry of emotions. Some smiled; others wept, waving white handkerchiefs or straw hats. And there was Rupert, not entirely alone anymore, for he had William. The young boy waved enthusiastically with both hands, shouting "bon voyage!" His innocent gesture, bought for 6 shillings, held a value far greater than any currency. It transformed Rupert's journey from one of isolation to a memorable departure, filled with a sense of connection and human warmth.

***

Even in the deepest solitude, a single act of kindness can ignite a spark of connection and hope. Like William's simple wave to Rupert Brooke, never underestimate the power of small gestures to touch hearts and transform moments of loneliness into memories of warmth and companionship. Let's embrace the art of small kindnesses, for they hold the power to create unforgettable impacts in our lives and the lives of others.

149. THE TRUE BLACK BELT

"Here is a test to find out whether your mission in life is complete. If you're alive, it isn't." – Richard Bach

A determined martial arts student knelt before his wise teacher, believing this was the day he would finally earn his Black Belt. Through endless training that pushed mind and body to the brink, he had proven his skill worthy of the highest honour.

"One final test remains," said the master. "You must answer: what is the true meaning of the Black Belt?"

"It is the culmination of my journey," the student replied proudly.

The master was silent. Then he spoke: "You are not yet ready. Return in one year."

The stunned student was left empty-handed. A year later, he knelt and gave a different response: "The Black Belt represents the pinnacle of excellence in our art." Again the master was silent, then sent him away.

One more year passed. Kneeling once more, the humbled student said: "I now see the Black Belt not as the end, but as the beginning – the start of a lifelong path of self-mastery."

The master nodded in approval. At last, the student understood that the true Black Belt is not a trophy to adorn on one's wall, but a commitment to continuous learning and effort without end. This wisdom had not been handed to him freely but hard-won through perseverance.

***

True mastery does not represent the completion of our development but instead marks the humble beginning of a lifetime of learning. Wisdom must be earned through patience and unending effort. The Black Belt symbolises not the end but the beginning of a lifelong journey of growth and excellence. Like the martial artist, recognise that true mastery lies in the constant pursuit of knowledge and improvement. Embrace each challenge as an opportunity to evolve, knowing that the path to greatness is endless.

150. THE BRIEF JOURNEY

"Life is short. Smile while you still have teeth."
– Mallory Hopkins

On a bustling city bus, a small yet significant interaction unfolded. A woman, burdened with numerous bags, climbed aboard and sat next to a man. As she settled in, her bags inadvertently hit him. The man, however, remained silent, absorbing the impact without a word of complaint.

Curious about his lack of reaction, the woman asked why he didn't express annoyance at being hit by her bags. The man's response was marked by a gentle smile and profound wisdom. He said, "There is no need to be upset about something so insignificant, as our journey together is so short. I'm getting off at the next stop."

This simple yet profound statement left a deep impression on the woman. His attitude reflected the importance of patience, understanding, and the choice to not sweat the small stuff.

***

Life is a series of brief journeys. The wisdom from the man on the bus reminds us to choose patience and understanding, recognising the fleeting nature of our interactions. Remember, the significance of our reactions often outweighs the trivialities that provoke them. Choose kindness and patience, for our journey together is indeed short.

CONCLUSION

This compilation of 150 stories has taken us on a profound journey across lives, lands, and the full spectrum of human experience. We uncovered timeless wisdom but also modern applications to current challenges. Several key themes have emerged which tie these multifaceted narratives together.

The stories emphasise that true progress comes from the right response to adversity, not its absence. Hardships play a pivotal role in awakening our hitherto unknown capabilities and resilience. Many tales underscore that societal and systemic change begins with transforming our individual mindsets and actions first. They highlight the importance of looking beyond external appearances to recognise the inherent worth in all people, regardless of status.

The narratives spotlight the significance of our beliefs and perceptions in shaping our reality. They encourage us to re-examine our assumptions, kerb impulsive reactions, approach situations with empathy and seek to understand context before judging others. We find that moral integrity carries more lasting rewards than compromised principles or superficial successes. Vitally, the stories underline that a meaningful life encompasses more than material achievements; it requires nurturing our relationships and leaving a compassionate legacy. As we reach the end of this literary journey, we part not only with insights but also deeper connections to the richness of human experience across space and time. These stories form strands that bind us beyond surface differences. They reveal that inside each person lies a story complex and unique, yet also universal. Fundamentally, the tales underscore the elemental truth that how we decide to live and relate to one another matters profoundly. Our choices ripple outwards influencing not just our own destinies but also the lives of generations to follow.

ACKNOWLEDGEMENTS

As stated profoundly by Ed Sabol, "Tell me a fact and I'll learn. Tell me the truth and I'll believe. But tell me a story and it will live in my heart forever." I have made it my mission to gather inspirational stories from wherever they may originate.

Many of these stories and anecdotes have been recounted from published works across numerous books, magazines, newspapers, other periodicals, and other social media posts. Some have been passed down through generations as oral histories while others found inspiration from speeches and adaptations of existing source material.

Attempts were made to credit all original authors. However, records of sources were not exhaustive, and some narratives have ambiguous origins. I extend my sincere gratitude to all contributors to this compilation, whether explicitly acknowledged or not.

Specific individuals whose work significantly influenced my collection include master storytellers Aesop and Anthony P. Castle alongside authors Barry Powell, Clare Edwards, Dan Clark, Dominic Mathews, Frank Mihalic, G. Francis Xavier, Gerard Fuller, Graham Twelftree, Hedwig Lewis, Jason Navallo, Jeannie Ingrham, Kevin Johnson, Krisanta Bella, M.K. Paul, Michal Stawicki, Philip Baker, Swami Sukhabodhananda, Mathew Vellankal and nameless creators on social media.

I extend my profound gratitude to the distinguished luminaries, accomplished achievers, and pioneering trailblazers — both men and women — who have profoundly impacted our world. Your enduring legacies and remarkable contributions continue to inspire and guide generations. You serve as exemplary role models, embodying virtues and achievements that motivate and uplift our current generation. I am honoured to have the opportunity to narrate your stories, celebrating your heroic deeds and remarkable accomplishments, and to share these narratives with the world, ensuring your impactful lives are rightfully acknowledged and remembered.

I extend profound thanks to Dr. (Fr) Joy Kachappilly, Rector, Assam Don Bosco University, Azara Campus, Guwahati, India, for writing the Foreword to the book and for constant encouragement and support. I am grateful to my Parents and Brother-Priests – Fr. George Parankimalil (Germany). Fr. Peter Parankimalil, MSFS (Assam), Fr. Antony Parankimalil, VC (Rwanda), who are my strength and inspiration. The unwavering support and love of my family members have been the cornerstone of my ventures.

My sincere appreciation goes to Notion Press Publishing House, and the entire team at Notion Press Publishing for their generosity, enthusiasm, and efficiency in publishing and expeditiously printing this book.

It is my earnest aspiration that this anthology will uplift readers while standing the test of time as an enduring wellspring of motivation, comfort and wisdom.

John Parankimalil,
Author

GENERAL INDEX

C

D

E

F

J

K

L

SUGGESTED RESOURCES

101 Inspiring Stories and Metaphors for Business and Life | Clare Edwards

99 Inspiring Stories for Presentations | Barry Powell

99 Perseverance Success Stories | Michal Stawicki

Collection of Inspiring and Motivational Stories | Krisanta Bella

Drive the Point Home | Graham Twelftree

From Humour to Inspiration | Mathew Vellankal

He Can Who Thinks He Can | John Parankimalil

Heart Speak Series (1 to 5) | Joji Valli

Insights | Jose Kaimlett

Inspirational Stories for Purposeful Living 1, 2 & 3 | John Parankimalil

Inspirational Stories, Series | G. Francis Xavier

Live Another Day | Deepu Paul

Stories for all Seasons | Gerard Fuller

The Millennium Stories | Frank Mihalic, SVD

The Next 500 Stories | Frank Mihalic, SVD

Tonic for the Heart 1, 2, 3 | Frank Mihalic

www.ingramcontent.com/pod-product-compliance
Lightning Source LLC
LaVergne TN
LVHW090130160826
845673LV00017B/1388